REA's Interactive Flashcards®

EMT-Basic

Emergency Medical Technician-Basic Exam

D0071409

Jeffrey Lindsey, Ph.D.
Fire Chief for Estero Fire Rescue
Estero, FL

Research & Education Association
Visit our website at
www.rea.com

The information contained herein presents scenarios and other narrative consistent with targeted preparation for the EMT-Basic Exam. The book's contents are deemed to be accurate and relevant to the cited subject matter at the time of publication. Neither the publisher, Research & Education Association, Inc., nor the author(s) is engaged in nor shall be construed as offering legal, nursing, or medical advice or assistance or a plan of care. If legal, nursing, or medical assistance is required, the services of a competent professional person should be sought.

Research & Education Association
61 Ethel Road West
Piscataway, New Jersey 08854
E-mail: info@rea.com

REA's Interactive Flashcards® Book for the EMT-Basic Exam

Published 2011

Printed in the United States of America

Library of Congress Control Number 2005931114

ISBN-13: 978-0-7386-0123-6
ISBN-10: 0-7386-0123-3

About the Author

Jeffrey Lindsey, Ph.D., has served in a variety of roles in the fire and EMS arena for the past 25 years. He has held positions as firefighter, paramedic, dispatcher, educator, coordinator, deputy chief, and chief. He has also worked in the insurance industry in education and risk control. Dr. Lindsey serves on various advisory boards, state and national committees, and also writes a monthly column for *JEMS*, a national EMS journal. He is the education coordinator for 24-7 EMS Videos and is currently the Operations Chief for Estero Fire Rescue in Estero, Florida. Dr. Lindsey is Senior Partner with International Consulting and Training Specialists.

He started his career in Carlisle, Pennsylvania, as a volunteer firefighter/EMT. In 1985, Dr. Lindsey pioneered the first advanced life support service in Cumberland County, Pennsylvania. Dr. Lindsey has experience in various environments, from the Philadelphia Fire Department to hospital and third service organization.

He holds an associate's degree in paramedicine from Harrisburg Area Community College, a bachelor's degree in Fire and Safety from the University of Cincinnati, a master's degree in Instructional Technology, and a Ph.D. in Instructional Technology/Adult Education from the University of South Florida. Dr. Lindsey is completing the Executive Fire Officer Program at the National Fire Academy.

He has designed and developed various courses in fire and EMS. Dr. Lindsey is accredited with the Chief Fire Officer Designation. He also is a certified Fire Officer II, Fire Instructor III, and paramedic in the state of Florida and holds a paramedic certificate for the state of Pennsylvania. He is a certified instructor in ACLS, Advanced Haz Mat Life Support, and PHTLS, and instructs a variety of courses.

REA's Interactive Flashcards®
EMT-Basic

What they're for and how to use them

Being an Emergency Medical Technician is an exciting, rewarding career, and REA wants you to succeed on the EMT-Basic Exam so you can be certified. Wherever you take your test to become an EMT, you'll find this flashcard book to be perfect for self-study, for reference, or just for a quick review.

This book is fact-packed! Each page contains targeted EMT professional questions that are simply the best way to check your "test readiness." Studying for an EMT exam with the unique features of flashcards in a book format makes your test preparation easier. There are no loose cards to misplace or lose. The cards are always in order for easier, more organized study. Study smarter using the unique interactive feature not found in other flashcards. Write your answer to a card's question on the front, and then compare it to the answer on the back.

The complete subject index gives you fast access to the full range of EMT-Basic topics. Bonus material throughout the book explores the history of EMTs, the types of situations EMTs respond to, and the current state of the growing EMT profession.

A tremendous amount of consideration and effort went into making this study aid the best of its kind. It is my hope that you will find this book to be an invaluable reference for your EMT studies.

Larry B. Kling
Chief Editor

Icon Key

Use these handy icons to locate questions by subject:

Airway & Breathing

Questions about the human pulmonary system which includes breathing, the mouth, nose, trachea, and the lungs

Cardiology

Questions about the heart, particularly the structure, function, and disorders of the heart.

Medical

Questions about medical practices, treatments, and procedures

Obstetrics & Pediatrics

Obstetrics questions focus on the care of women during pregnancy, childbirth, and the recuperative period following delivery. Pediatrics questions deal with the care of infants and children.

Trauma

Questions about serious injuries, severe shocks to the body, and appropriate medical treatment

Questions

Q–1

You arrive to find a 48-year-old male complaining that his chest feels heavy. The patient is awake and talking to you. During your assessment you note that his skin is pale, cool, and clammy. Your first step is to

(A) apply your AED.

(B) administer supplemental oxygen.

(C) obtain a past medical history.

(D) assist the patient in taking his neighbor's nitroglycerin.

Your Answer _____

_____

Career Pulse

Helpful websites:
NAEMT (National Association of EMTs)
www.neemt.org
NREMT (National Registry of Emergency
Medical Technicians) www.nremt.org

Correct Answers

A–1

(B) Your first step is to administer supplemental oxygen. When treating chest pain it is important to get oxygen to the patient as soon as possible to help alleviate damage to the heart muscle.

Questions

Which of the following is the correct flow of blood through the heart and lungs?

(A) inferior/superior vena cavae, lungs, right atrium, left atrium, right ventricle, left ventricle, aorta

(B) inferior/superior vena cavae, left atrium, left ventricle, lungs, right atrium, left ventricle, aorta

(C) inferior/superior vena cavae, lungs, aorta, left atrium, left ventricle, right atrium, left ventricle

(D) inferior/superior vena cavae, right atrium, right ventricle, lungs, left atrium, left ventricle, aorta

Your Answer _____

_____

Correct Answers

A–2

(D) The blood returns from the body to the heart through the inferior/superior vena cavae, to the right atrium, to the right ventricle. It then goes through the pulmonary artery to the lungs and is oxygenated. From there it returns to the left atrium through the pulmonary vein. From the left atrium it goes to the left ventricle and back out to the body through the aorta.

Questions

The mitral or bicuspid valve

(A) prevents blood from backflowing into the left atrium.

(B) prevents blood from backflowing into the right atrium.

(C) prevents the blood from backflowing into the lungs.

(D) is located between the left atrium and the right ventricle.

Your Answer _____

_____

Fast Fact

EMTs and paramedics work both indoors and outdoors in all types of weather, and are required to do considerable kneeling, bending and heavy lifting.

Correct Answers

A–3

(A) The mitral or bicuspid valve is located between the left atrium and the left ventricle. It prevents the blood from backflowing into the left atrium.

Questions

The electrical impulse generated in the right atrium is called the

(A) atrioventricular node.

(B) purkinje fibers.

(C) sinoatrial node.

(D) bundle of his.

Your Answer _____

Which component of blood provides an immune system for the body, defending against infections?

(A) red blood cells

(B) white blood cells

(C) plasma

(D) platelets

Your Answer _____

Correct Answers

A–4

(C) The electrical impulse generated at the right atrium is the sinoatrial node (SA node). It travels through both atria, causing both to contract simultaneously, which propels the blood to the ventricles.

A–5

(B) White blood cells provide part of the body's immune system, or defense against infections. Red blood cells give blood its color and transport the oxygen to the body's cells and carbon dioxide away from the body's cells. Plasma is the serum, or fluid, that carries blood cells and nutrients to the body's cells. Platelets are important in the formation of blood clots.

Questions

When differentiating between angina pectoris and a myocardial infarction, you know that

(A) there is no difference between the two.

(B) angina pectoris is caused by physical or emotional stress.

(C) rest will relieve symptoms of a myocardial infarction.

(D) the pain from angina pectoris is continual and will not go away.

Your Answer _____

_____

Correct Answers

A–6

(B) Angina pectoris is usually caused by a physical or emotional state of stress. It usually only lasts from 3 to 8 minutes, but no longer than 10 minutes. It is usually relieved by rest, unlike a myocardial infarction.

Questions

911

You arrive on the scene to discover an unconscious patient. Upon completing your initial assessment, you find the patient to be pulseless and apneic. Your next step would be to

(A) begin CPR.

(B) give two ventilations.

(C) apply the AED.

(D) check the pulse for another 60 seconds.

Your Answer _____

_____

Career Pulse

Employment of EMTs and paramedics is expected to grow faster than the average for all occupations through 2012.

Correct Answers

911

(C) The first step in an unconscious, pulseless, apneic patient is to apply the AED. It is important to deliver a counter-shock with the AED if the patient is in v-fib or pulseless v-tach.

Questions

The AED is used to treat patients in

(A) asystole.

(B) ventricular tachycardia with a pulse.

(C) ventricular fibrillation.

(D) pulseless electrical activity.

Your Answer _____

_____

Which of the following is the first line of defense in fighting against infectious disease?

(A) vaccinations

(B) hand washing

(C) using BSI

(D) using 100% bleach

Your Answer _____

_____

Correct Answers

A–8

(C) The AED is designed to treat patients in v-fib or pulseless v-tach. The AED should only be connected to patients that are pulseless and apneic. The AED is designed to shock those electrical rhythms that are disorganized or very fast and do not have pulses associated with them.

A–9

(B) The most fundamental process and the first line of protection against infectious disease is hand washing. Vaccinations and BSI are important components of preventing infectious diseases, but hand washing is the most fundamental and first line of protection.

Questions

911

You arrive on the scene to discover a 65-year-old female lying on the floor of her living room. Your first step in the care of this patient is to

(A) begin chest compressions.

(B) apply the AED.

(C) maintain an open airway.

(D) assess level of consciousness.

Your Answer _____

_____

Fast Fact

EMTs and paramedics may be exposed to diseases such as hepatitis-B and AIDS, as well as violence from drug overdose victims or mentally unstable patients.

Correct Answers

A–10

911

(D) The first step when arriving at the patient's side is to establish the patient's level of responsiveness.

Questions

You are on the scene with a patient dying from a terminal illness. The spouse of the patient begins to verbally attack you. Which emotional stage is this individual exhibiting?

(A) denial

(B) anger

(C) bargaining

(D) depression

Your Answer _____

_____

Correct Answers

A–11

(B) As the dying patient and/or the patient's family moves through the stages of emotion, you may find yourself in the middle of the situation. In this case the patient's family is really not angry at you, but exhibiting the signs of anger commonly found at this stage in the process.

Questions

You arrive on the scene to find a patient who had a productive cough for the past two weeks. The patient is complaining of a fever and night sweats. Your next step would be to

(A) obtain a better medical history.

(B) obtain vital signs.

(C) immediately transport the patient to the hospital.

(D) put your HEPA mask on.

Your Answer _____

_____

Career Pulse

The National Registry of EMTs (NREMT) is a private, central certifying entity, with individual states usually setting their own standards of licensure. [http://en.wikipedia.org/wiki/Paramedic]

Correct Answers

A–12

(D) A patient with a productive cough for any length of time should be suspect for TB. Nonetheless, a mask is an important universal precaution for any patient with a productive cough to prevent the spread of any airborne infectious disease.

Questions

You arrive on scene, finding an unconscious patient. There are no other individuals in the vicinity to give you any information or permission to treat the patient. Even though the patient cannot give you consent to treat him, you begin to do so because of

(A) expressed consent.

(B) implied consent.

(C) advanced directives.

(D) emergency consent.

Your Answer _____

_____

Correct Answers

(B) Implied consent occurs when you assume that a patient who is unresponsive or unable to make a rational decision would consent to life-saving emergency care.

Questions

Q–14

You arrive at an emergency room to find that the nurses are busy taking care of other patients. You are getting off shift and want to get back to your base station. You and your partner move the patient into a hospital bed, lay the report on the bed with the patient, and leave. You and your partner have just committed

(A) abandonment.

(B) negligence.

(C) appropriate patient care.

(D) vicarious liability.

Your Answer _____

_____

Fast Fact

At the scene of an emergency, EMTs and paramedics determine the nature and extent of the patient's condition while trying to ascertain whether the patient has preexisting medical problems.

Correct Answers

(A) Abandonment is any time you stop caring for a patient without ensuring the patient receives equal or better care. Giving a verbal patient report coupled with a caregiver of equal or greater level of care is imperative for appropriate patient transfer of care and the avoidance of abandonment.

Questions

Q-15

Which of the following is NOT an appropriate scenario to give patient information?

(A) another health care worker needs the information to continue medical care

(B) information is required for billing purposes

(C) your neighbor asks what was wrong with the patient

(D) you are subpoenaed in court

Your Answer _____

_____

Q-16

Which artery do you typically assess on an infant?

(A) brachial artery

(B) carotid artery

(C) femoral artery

(D) radial artery

Your Answer _____

_____

Correct Answers

A–15

(C) There are few instances when you can give patient information to anyone. Patient information is confidential. You may give patient information to another health care provider to continue medical care, law enforcement as part of an investigation, third-party billing form, or by a legal subpoena.

A–16

(A) The brachial artery is the best place to assess the pulse on any patient under the age of one. It is difficult to assess the carotid because these patients typically do not have a neck and the radial is not reliable. The brachial is the pronounced site to assess for a pulse.

Questions

The condition in which a patient has a high level of sugar in his blood is called

(A) hypoglycemia.

(B) diabetes.

(C) hyperglycemia.

(D) hyperkalemia.

Your Answer _____

911

You arrive on the scene of a patient who fell from a ladder. You should open the patient's airway by using

(A) head-tilt/chin-lift.

(B) jaw-thrust maneuver.

(C) neck-lift/head-tilt.

(D) head-tilt/jaw-thrust.

Your Answer _____

Correct Answers

A–17

(C) A patient who has a high sugar level in their blood may have diabetes. However, this is the definition of hyperglycemia. Hypoglycemia is low blood sugar. Hyperglycemia is a lack of insulin and sugar cannot enter the cells. Therefore, it remains in the bloodstream, causing a high level of sugar in the blood.

A–18

(B) Care should be taken when opening an airway in a patient with a possible or suspected head or neck injury. The jaw-thrust maneuver is the choice in opening an airway in these patients. This keeps the head in a neutral position and does not put any undue stress on the cervical spine.

Questions

911

Arriving on the scene to find an unresponsive patient, the patient begins to vomit. You turn on your suction unit and prepare to suction. You should apply suction

(A) as you insert the catheter.

(B) by alternating every 5 seconds between inserting and withdrawing the catheter.

(C) while withdrawing the catheter, and for no more than 15 seconds.

(D) while inserting and withdrawing the catheter.

Your Answer _____

Career Pulse

Population growth and urbanization will increase the demand for full-time paid EMTs and paramedics rather than for volunteers.

Correct Answers

911

(C) Suction should only be applied when you withdraw the catheter. Suctioning should only last for 15 seconds. Patients become hypoxic during the suctioning process and need to be ventilated or supplied with oxygen for a 2-minute period between suctioning.

Questions

911

You are treating a choking victim when he loses consciousness. You assist the patient to the floor. Your next step should be to

(A) attempt to ventilate the patient.

(B) perform five abdominal thrusts.

(C) establish responsiveness.

(D) begin CPR.

Your Answer _____

_____

Correct Answers

A–20

911

(D) Once the patient becomes unresponsive, you need to activate the emergency response system and begin CPR. Since you are the emergency response system, you would immediately begin CPR.

Questions

When assessing a 35-year-old patient complaining she is short of breath, you note that her breathing is in excess of 28 times per minute. This is considered

(A) neuropnea.

(B) apnea.

(C) bradypnea.

(D) tachypnea.

Your Answer _____

Correct Answers

A–21

(D) Respiratory rates greater than 20 breaths per minute are considered tachypnea. Less than 12 breaths per minute are bradypnea and absent breathing is apnea.

Questions

911

A 27-year-old patient is involved in a motor vehicle accident. You attempt to ventilate the patient, but realize you cannot open the patient's jaw due to trauma. Your technique of ventilating the patient would be

(A) mouth-to-mouth technique.

(B) mouth-to-mouth and nose technique.

(C) mouth-to-nose technique.

(D) a Combitube.

Your Answer _____

_____

Fast Fact

Some paramedics are trained to treat patients with minor injuries on the scene of an accident or at their home without transporting them to a medical facility.

Correct Answers

911

(C) Mouth-to-nose technique is the ideal method for this patient. Anytime you have a patient that has severe soft tissue or bone injury around the mouth, or you cannot open the mouth, or cannot get a good seal around the mouth, the mouth-to-nose technique is the preferred choice for ventilation.

Questions

911

The proper way to ventilate an adult patient is to either administer oxygen through a bag-valve mask or by mouth-to-mouth. You also want to deliver each breath or ventilation over a one-second period. This will

(A) reduce the chance of gastric distention.

(B) prevent hyperoxygenation.

(C) prevent hypoxia.

(D) prevent using too much air or oxygen.

Your Answer _____

_____

Correct Answers

911

(A)   One concern when ventilating an adult patient with a BVM or by mouth-to-mouth is to deliver the ventilation over a one-second time period. This aids in reducing gastric distention by not forcing air or oxygen into the esophagus and inflating the stomach with air. Remember, what goes into the stomach must come out. Air rises, hence over time the air you put into the stomach will come back out with whatever gastric contents the patient has in her stomach.

Questions

Q–24

The appropriate rate to ventilate a seven-year-old patient is

(A) one breath every 1 to 3 seconds.

(B) one breath every 2 to 4 seconds.

(C) one breath every 3 to 5 seconds.

(D) one breath every 4 to 6 seconds.

Your Answer _____

_____

Career Pulse

Competition for jobs in local rescue squad departments will be greater than in private ambulance services.

Correct Answers

A–24

(C) The appropriate rate to ventilate a seven-year-old would be one breath every three to five seconds.

Questions

$\boxed{911}$

Which of the following is NOT a consideration when treating a fall victim?

(A) distance the patient fell

(B) height of the ladder

(C) surface upon which the patient landed

(D) body part that impacted first

Your Answer _____

_____

Correct Answers

$$\boxed{911}$$

(B) How tall the ladder is does not make a significant difference in your assessment. The distance the patient fell is important to note because you would suspect different injuries from a patient who fell from the four foot area of a twelve foot ladder than if he had fallen from the top. The surface the patient landed on is always an important aspect to assess. If the patient fell in a sandy area, he would have different injuries than if he fell onto a concrete surface. The body part that impacted first would give you clues in your assessment of suspected injuries. If the patient landed on the buttocks, you would suspect lower back injuries versus if she had fallen on the back of her head, you would suspect head and neck injuries.

Questions

You are treating a patient with shortness of breath. You want to deliver 6 liters per minute of oxygen. You would deliver this flow rate with a

(A) nasal cannula.

(B) simple face mask.

(C) partial re-breather.

(D) non-rebreather.

Your Answer _____

_____

Correct Answers

A–26

(A) The nasal cannula is used when you want oxygen to flow at a rate of 1 to 6 L/min. A nasal cannula delivers a concentration of oxygen in the range of 24 to 44 percent.

Questions

911

Your unit is the first to arrive on the scene of a motor vehicle accident. As you are approaching the scene you notice the vehicle has struck a pole and that there are electrical lines down on the vehicle. The patient appears to be unresponsive. Your first action should be to

(A) remove the electrical lines.

(B) call the electric company and keep everyone, including emergency personnel, away from the car.

(C) don rubber boots and approach the car carefully.

(D) remove the victim from the car immediately, since she is unresponsive.

Your Answer _____

_____

Correct Answers

$$\boxed{911}$$

(B) The first step at any scene is scene safety. Electrical lines on the vehicle are unsafe. It is your responsibility to secure the scene by not allowing anyone to approach the vehicle until the power company arrives and determines the scene is safe. Under no circumstances should you ever play the role of any utility company.

Questions

Your patient responds to your verbal commands, such as "Open your eyes" or "Squeeze my hand." This patient's level of consciousness is classified as

(A) **A** — **A**lert.

(B) **V** — **R**esponds to Verbal stimulus.

(C) **P** — **R**esponds to Painful stimulus.

(D) **U** — Unresponsive.

Your Answer _____

_____

Fast Fact

Emergency treatment for complicated problems is carried out by EMTs under the direction of medical doctors by radio preceding or during transport.

Correct Answers

A–28

(B) Using the mnemonic AVPU, this patient would be classified as responds to **V**erbal stimulus. If the patient is awake, alert, speaks to you, and responds appropriately he would be considered **A**lert. If the patient is not alert, does not obey your commands or respond to voice, but does respond to your painful stimulus, he would be classified as responds to **P**ainful stimulus. If the patient does not respond to voice or painful stimulus then he is classified as **U**nresponsive.

Questions

When you auscultate the patient's lungs, you hear a harsh, high-pitched sound on inspiration. This sound is called

(A) snoring.

(B) gurgling.

(C) crowing.

(D) stridor.

Your Answer _____

_____

Correct Answers

A–29

(D) When you hear a harsh, high-pitched sound on inspiration, you can almost be certain you are hearing stridor. Crowing and stridor are very similar except that crowing is a sound more like a cawing crow. Stridor is typically associated with an upper airway problem as a result of an infection, allergic reaction, or burn.

Questions

In reference to the patient in the previous question, you know the harsh sound is indicative of

(A) complete airway obstruction.

(B) CHF.

(C) poor lung sounds.

(D) partial airway occlusion.

Your Answer _____

The normal respiratory rate for infants is

(A) 25 to 50 breaths per minute.

(B) 15 to 30 breaths per minute.

(C) 12 to 20 breaths per minute.

(D) 8 to 18 breaths per minute.

Your Answer _____

Correct Answers

A–30

(D) Since there is air that is still moving with a patient that has the sounds of stridor, the patient has a partial airway occlusion. Granted, the patient has poor lung sounds, but in this case the best and most appropriate answer is a partial airway occlusion.

A–31

(A) The normal respiratory rate for an infant is 25 to 50 breaths per minute. 15 to 30 breaths per minute is for a child and 12 to 20 breaths per minute is for an adult.

Questions

Q–32

Which of the following is not part of the focused history and physical exam?

(A) form a general impression of the patient

(B) take the patient's history

(C) conduct a physical exam

(D) take baseline vital signs

Your Answer _____

Q–33

911

You arrive on the scene of an incident where a sixteen-year-old male fell approximately 12 feet. This would be considered

(A) a trauma alert.

(B) a significant mechanism of injury.

(C) not a significant mechanism of injury.

(D) a case with a load 'n' go patient.

Your Answer _____

Correct Answers

A–32

(A) Forming a general impression of the patient is typically performed during the initial assessment. The focused history and physical exam is to identify any additional injuries or conditions that may also be life threatening.

A–33

(C) A patient over the age of eight is considered an adult for most medical care purposes. A fall of greater than 20 feet is considered a significant injury in adults. If this had been an infant or child, it would then have been a significant mechanism of injury since any fall greater than 10 feet would be considered a significant mechanism of injury.

Questions

911

During your assessment of a fall victim, you notice a clear fluid leaking from the ear that appears to be cerebral spinal fluid. This would signify that the patient may have a

(A) severe head injury.

(B) a ruptured ear drum.

(C) dislocated jaw.

(D) basilar skull fracture.

Your Answer _____

Career Pulse

EMT job opportunities will be best for those who have advanced certification.

Correct Answers

$$\boxed{911}$$

(A) This patient may have a basilar skull fracture but you cannot tell that from the limited information you received. The information provided does suggest that the patient has a severe head injury. A further exam would need to be conducted and the patient would need to get to definitive care quickly for a successful outcome.

Questions

911

You are assessing a 25-year-old male patient. During your assessment of the chest, you notice the patient has four ribs broken in two places. This type of injury is called a

(A) fractured chest.

(B) paradoxical movement.

(C) flailed segment.

(D) chest deformity.

Your Answer _____

_____

During your assessment of a patient's extremities, it is important to assess PMS. PMS stands for:

(A) pulses, major bleeding, sensation

(B) posterior, medial, sweep

(C) pulses, motor function, sensation

(D) pooling, motor sensation, senses

Your Answer _____

_____

Correct Answers

A–35

911

(C) This is a classic indicator of a flailed segment, which is when there are three or more ribs broken in two places. Paradoxical motion, another indicator of a flailed segment, is when the flailed segment sinks in when the patient inhales.

A–36

(C) After inspecting and palpating the patient's extremities, it is essential to check each extremity for **P**ulses, **M**otor function, and **S**ensation.

Questions

Which of the following pulse pressures is considered narrow?

(A) 30

(B) 20

(C) 40

(D) 35

Your Answer _____

911

When assessing a trauma patient, you should conduct a SAMPLE history

(A) immediately.

(B) a SAMPLE history is not necessary in a trauma patient.

(C) as part of the focused or ongoing survey.

(D) following the rapid trauma assessment.

Your Answer _____

Correct Answers

A–37

(B) A pulse pressure less than 30 is considered a narrow pulse pressure. The pulse pressure is the difference between the systolic and the diastolic blood pressure.

A–38

(D) The SAMPLE history should be taken after the rapid trauma assessment. If two EMT-B's are working together, it may be acceptable to take the SAMPLE as part of the rapid trauma assessment. It is important to take a SAMPLE history in every patient. This will reveal past medical history that may be pertinent to the treatment you administer.

Questions

911

As you are assessing the patient, you recognize that the patient has an inadequate breathing rate. Your next step should be to

(A) continue your assessment.

(B) stop your assessment and administer the appropriate amount of oxygen.

(C) reassess the patient.

(D) take the patient's vital signs.

Your Answer _____

_____

Fast Fact

In an emergency, EMTs and paramedics are typically dispatched to the scene by a 911 operator.

Correct Answers

A–39

911

(B) Breathing is part of the ABC's. Immediately upon identifying that the patient has an inadequate breathing rate, you should administer the appropriate amount of oxygen. If your partner is not doing anything critical at this point, you can direct him or her to administer the oxygen.

Questions

911

Which of the following is NOT part of the trauma score?

(A) age of the patient

(B) respiratory rate

(C) systolic blood pressure

(D) Glasgow coma score

Your Answer _____

In which age range is capillary refill most useful?

(A) infants only

(B) patients less than 6-years-old

(C) patients greater than 6-years-old

(D) all ages

Your Answer _____

Correct Answers

A–40

$\boxed{911}$

(A) The age of the patient is not part of the trauma score. The three major components of the trauma score are the respiratory rate, the systolic blood pressure, and the Glasgow coma score. There may be other components depending on which text you read, but these are typically the major components and age is not found in any of the trauma scores.

A–41

(B) Capillary refill is most useful in patients less than 6 years of age. Capillary refill may be assessed in every patient, but it typically is not a reliable indicator in patients over the age of 6.

Questions

Q–42

You are assessing a conscious patient complaining of chest pain. Which mnemonic will assist you in assessing the patient's current chief complaint?

(A) DCAPP BTLS

(B) SAMPLE

(C) OPQRST

(D) ABC

Your Answer _____

_____

Q–43

You are treating an unresponsive patient. Vital signs should be taken every

(A) 15 minutes.

(B) 10 minutes.

(C) 5 minutes.

(D) 2 minutes.

Your Answer _____

_____

Correct Answers

A–42

(**C**) OPQRST is a good mnemonic to assess the current patient's chief complaint. SAMPLE is geared more toward the patient's history and should still be used in the assessment of the patient, but it is not the most appropriate mnemonic in this scenario. Since the patient is conscious, the ABCs are already taken care of, plus the ABCs do not necessarily provide you with the best history of the current chief complaint. DCAPP BTLS is used primarily to assess a trauma patient.

A–43

(**C**) Any patient that is classified as critical or unstable should have vital signs taken every 5 minutes. An unresponsive patient is considered a critical or unstable patient; hence the vital signs should be taken every 5 minutes. In stable patients the vital signs should be taken every 15 minutes.

Questions

Q-44

911

During your transport to the hospital the patient seems to be getting worse. You should

(A) reassess the patient.

(B) turn off the oxygen.

(C) ask the driver to go faster.

(D) call the hospital and notify them.

Your Answer _____

_____

Q-45

As part of your OPQRST assessment, you ask the patient how bad the pain is. To which part of the OPQRST would this question relate?

(A) provocation

(B) quality

(C) radiation

(D) severity

Your Answer _____

_____

Correct Answers

A–44

911

(A) Any time the patient's condition changes, you should immediately reassess the patient. After reassessing the patient you may need to alter your treatment accordingly. It may be necessary to notify the hospital of the patient's change in condition, but this should occur after your re-assessment. Speed of the vehicle should never be increased to jeopardize the safety of the crew, the patient, and those around the ambulance.

A–45

(D) "How bad is the pain?" would relate to severity in the OPQRST part of the assessment. Asking "What makes the symptom worse?" would be provocation. "How would you describe the pain?" would be quality. "Where do you feel the pain?" or "Where does the pain go?" would be the radiation portion.

Questions

You are treating a 70-year-old female with shortness of breath. This patient may be suffering from

(A) congestive heart failure.

(B) a heart attack.

(C) pneumonia.

(D) all of the above

Your Answer _____

_____

When communicating on the radio, you should always

(A) talk louder than your normal voice.

(B) give as much detailed information as possible.

(C) keep your information short and to the point.

(D) use codes to confuse the public.

Your Answer _____

_____

Correct Answers

A–46

(D) It is difficult to determine from the limited information exactly what the patient is suffering from. Geriatric patients do not always present clear-cut signs and symptoms as younger patients. A geriatric patient with shortness of breath could be suffering from emphysema, congestive heart failure, chronic bronchitis, pulmonary embolism, pneumonia, pulmonary edema, heart attack, or asthma. You need to remember to treat the symptoms and continue to do a thorough assessment.

A–47

(C) When using the radio to communicate, you want to keep your messages brief and to the point. It is not necessary to talk louder than normal. You should talk as you normally do and avoid codes or language that may confuse even the most experienced radio operator. Plain English is acceptable language for radio communications.

Questions

Q–48

You are treating an 80-year-old female. The patient is on a variety of medications for a variety of illnesses. The patient is difficult to arouse, her pupils are constricted, and her breathing is shallow. You should suspect

(A) a heart attack.

(B) a drug overdose.

(C) seizures.

(D) a stroke.

Your Answer _____

Career Pulse

EMTs and paramedics use special equipment, such as backboards, to immobilize patients before placing them on stretchers and securing them in the ambulance.

Correct Answers

A–48

(B) Any of these could be indicative of the patient's condition, however none of these symptoms are typical except for the drug overdose. Many geriatric patients take numerous medications, and it is not uncommon to forget when they took their medication last, or they may a have difficult time telling which pill is for what. Drug overdoses should be considered with these patients, but it is also important that you do a thorough assessment and treat the signs and symptoms you see.

Questions

911

The most important information to know when responding to a call is

(A) the location of the patient and his phone number.

(B) the nature of the call and the location.

(C) the location of the call and the number of patients.

(D) the number of patients and the nature of the call.

Your Answer _____

Correct Answers

$$\boxed{911}$$

(B)   The nature of the call and the location are the most important initial factors you need. First, you need to know where the call is located, so you can begin to respond to the call. Second, it is important to know the nature of the call so you can begin to plan your strategy for handling the call when you arrive on the scene. It is good to know the number of patients at the scene, but it is not the most critical at this point because in most incidents you will be able to get that information through the nature of the call.

Questions

Which of the following medications is an EMT-B not allowed to assist the patient in taking?

(A) the neighbor's nitroglycerin for chest pain

(B) an albuterol inhaler for shortness of breath

(C) the patient's nitroglycerin for chest pain

(D) the patient's epi pen for an allergic reaction

Your Answer _____

_____

Which of the following statements should you avoid writing on your patient care report form?

(A) The patient's mother stated she is HIV positive.

(B) The patient's pain was not relieved by nitro-glycerin.

(C) The patient acted like he was drunk during the assessment.

(D) The patient was out of the vehicle walking around upon your arrival.

Your Answer _____

_____

Correct Answers

A–50

(A) The EMT-B can assist a patient with the patient's inhaler, nitroglycerin, and their epinephrine pen as long the patient's condition warrants it and they have received approval from their medical director. In no circumstance should the patient be given any medication other than their own.

A–51

(C) Your patient care report should reflect objective findings. Writing subjective findings such as the patient appeared drunk is not appropriate. Any time you have a subjective opinion you should avoid writing it on your patient care report. It is acceptable to write the patient is HIV positive. Keep in mind this is a medical legal report and part of the patient findings. It could also affect treatment once you arrive at the hospital. Pertinent negatives are also important to document. It is just as important to know when a medication or treatment doesn't work the same as when it does.

Questions

911

You are working a motor vehicle accident. You have three patients. Two of these patients do not want any medical treatment nor do they want transport. The third patient is injured and needs to be immobilized and transported to the hospital. How should you handle the two patients NOT wanting medical care or treatment?

(A) Have law enforcement take care of the two individuals.

(B) Transport the patient to the hospital; there is nothing else needed for the two individuals since they are not injured and do not want care.

(C) Request a second unit to respond and handle these individuals.

(D) Have your partner secure a signed refusal for each patient.

Your Answer _____

_____

Correct Answers

A–52

911

(D) Even though neither of these individuals is hurt nor requires transport to the hospital, it does not preclude you from getting a treatment and transport release form signed. All patient refusals need to be an informed decision and in writing. Depending on your patient's condition, you may need to call a second unit to get the refusals. However, nothing in this scenario suggests the patient is injured so badly that you or your partner could not get the refusals signed while the other EMT-B continues to assess and provide care for the injured patient.

Questions

When you are completing your patient care report, you write the wrong medication on the report. Which of the following is the acceptable way to correct the error?

(A) write over the word

(B) erase the word

(C) scratch the word out

(D) draw line through the error; date and initial it

Your Answer _____

Which medication that will open bronchioles and increase effectiveness of breathing is typically used to treat a patient with shortness of breath?

(A) bronchodilators

(B) bronchoconstrictors

(C) anti-inflammatory

(D) pneumodilator

Your Answer _____

Correct Answers

A–53

(D) When correcting errors on medical reports, the only acceptable way to correct an error is to draw a line through the error and initial it. It is not acceptable to try to erase it, write over it, use correction fluid, or scribble it out. This symbolizes that the person writing the report is trying to hide something, and should you be called into a court of law, this would not work in your favor. In most instances, the opposing lawyer would use it to their advantage.

A–54

(A) When treating a patient with shortness of breath, it is common to use a bronchodilator. A bronchodilator is designed to relax and dilate the bronchioles, which in turn increases the effectiveness of breathing and relieves the patient's signs and symptoms. A common bronchodilator is Albuterol.

Questions

You respond to a dispatch reporting a person with severe shortness of breath. Arriving on the scene, in what position would you expect to find the patient?

(A) lying in bed

(B) tripod position

(C) walking back and forth

(D) semi-fowler's position

Your Answer _____

Which of the following is not a contraindication for assisting a patient in the use of her bronchodilator inhaler?

(A) The patient is very lethargic.

(B) The patient has already taken an inhalation treatment.

(C) The inhaler is not prescribed to the patient.

(D) Medical direction has not authorized you to assist the patient.

Your Answer _____

Correct Answers

A–55

(B) Patients that are severely short of breath will most likely place themselves in a tripod position. They will be sitting with their hands out in front of them. They will be leaning forward slightly. Most patients who are short of breath will not tolerate lying down nor will they want to be in any position except for an upright sitting position.

A–56

(B) The contraindications for using an inhaler include a patient not responsive enough to use the Multi Dose Inhaler (MDI), the MDI is not prescribed for the patient, permission has not been granted by medical direction, and the patient has already taken the maximum allowed dose prior to your arrival. This patient has taken one dose, but in most instances patients may take multiple inhalation treatments. It is always important to contact medical direction and get approval to assist in administering any patient's medication.

Questions

You are assessing a 56-year-old female. On examination you note the patient has a thin, barrel-shaped chest and diminished breath sounds with wheezes and rhonchi on exhalation. She purses her lips when she breaths. Her skin is cool and clammy with a pink complexion. Her breathing rate is about 28 times per minute. You would suspect this patient is suffering from

(A) congestive heart failure.

(B) emphysema.

(C) asthma.

(D) bronchitis.

Your Answer _____

_____

Fast Fact

The NAEMT (National Association of Emergency Medical Technicians) is the oldest and largest EMS association in America representing all EMS personnel.

Correct Answers

(B) This patient has typical signs and symptoms associated with emphysema. Patients who are suffering from emphysema may also have a prolonged exhalation, extreme difficulty of breathing on exertion, tachycardia, and in some instances may be on home oxygen.

Questions

Q–58

Status asthmaticus is defined as

(A) any patient with severe respiratory distress.

(B) patients who cannot tolerate oxygen.

(C) a severe, prolonged asthmatic attack.

(D) an asthma attack not relieved by the MDI.

Your Answer _____

Q–59

COPD patients may develop a condition character-ized by a constantly high carbon dioxide level in the blood due to poor gas exchange. This may cause the cell receptors to respond to low levels of oxygen to stimulate breathing. This condition is called

(A) hypoxic drive.

(B) anaerobic drive.

(C) oxygen deficiency.

(D) asthma.

Your Answer _____

Correct Answers

A–58

(C)   Status asthmaticus is a severe, prolonged asthmatic attack. It is an acute attack that involves airway obstruction, due to bronchospasm, swelling of mucous membranes in the bronchi walls, and plugging of bronchi by thick mucous secretions. An allergic reaction or emotional stress may bring on these attacks.

A–59

(A)   COPD patients may develop a hypoxic drive. This is a result of a constantly high carbon dioxide level in the blood from poor gas exchange, which causes the cell receptors to respond to low levels of oxygen to stimulate breathing. This is the theory behind not giving a COPD patient too much oxygen. Typically, a COPD patient should be administered 2–3 L/min of oxygen via nasal cannula. It is acceptable to increase the oxygen in emergency situations. Refer to your local protocols for any deviation from this guideline.

Questions

You are treating a 22-year-old female at the local supermarket. The patient is short of breath. The patient stated that it came on suddenly and is a sharp, stabbing pain in the left side of her chest. She is breathing about 26 times per minute. Her skin is cool and clammy. She is very restless and anxious. The only medication she states that she takes is birth control pills. You should suspect

(A) ectopic pregnancy.

(B) heart attack.

(C) pulmonary embolism.

(D) asthma.

Your Answer _____

Correct Answers

A–60

(C) A pulmonary embolism is a common side effect of birth control pills. Classic signs of a pulmonary embolism include all the symptoms in the scenario plus a possible cough, tachypnea, tachycardia, syncope, decrease in blood pressure, cyanosis, and distended neck veins. Additional causes of pulmonary embolisms are surgery, prolonged immobilization, thrombophlebitis, certain medications, chronic atrial fibrillation, and multiple fractures.

Questions

Your patient is a diabetic. On conducting your SAMPLE, you find out that the patient took his insulin, but did not eat breakfast. The patient is alert enough to swallow. Your next step is to

(A) administer oxygen.

(B) administer oral glucose.

(C) administer insulin.

(D) contact medical direction.

Your Answer _____

Career Pulse

There are 4 levels of EMT training. An EMT-1 is trained to care for patients at the scene of an accident and while transporting patients by ambulance to the hospital under medical direction.

Correct Answers

A–61

(B) In this particular case, oral glucose is needed. The patient has taken his insulin but has not eaten; therefore he does not have any sugar for the insulin. If the patient is alert and can swallow, you would give him oral glucose. Depending on your local protocols you would not have to typically contact medical direction. If the patient becomes unresponsive or becomes less responsive, you would cease giving the oral glucose.

Questions

You are treating a 58-year-old female who had a brief episode of numbness on the left side of her body, a headache, difficulty swallowing, and a brief period of disorientation. She states the symptoms only lasted for about ten minutes. Now, she is just feeling a little weak and tired. She is most likely suffering from

(A) a heart attack.

(B) syncope.

(C) a cerebral vascular accident.

(D) a transient ischemic attack.

Your Answer _____

Correct Answers

(D) The symptoms of a transient ischemic attack (TIA) are similar to that of a cerebral vascular accident (CVA). The difference is TIA's usually only last no more than 5 – 10 minutes. An individual can typically have multiple TIA's. They also may not have all the symptoms of a CVA, but may have a few of the symptoms.

Questions

A person with high blood pressure will typically have what kind of stroke?

(A) occlusive

(B) thrombosis

(C) embolism

(D) hemorrhagic

Your Answer _____

The kidneys are located in the

(A) upper abdominal quadrant.

(B) peritoneum.

(C) lower abdominal quadrant.

(D) pelvic region.

Your Answer _____

Correct Answers

A-63

(D) Patients who have high blood pressure typically have a hemorrhagic stroke. This results from a rupture of an artery that causes bleeding within the brain or in the space around the outer surface of the brain. Persons that have hypertension typically have damaged arteries as a result of the hypertension, which leads to a higher susceptibility to a hemorrhagic stroke.

A-64

(B) The kidneys are located in a space called the peritoneum. This area is to the rear of the abdominal cavity and is sometimes referred to as the retroperitoneal area of the abdomen. Pain in the lower back may be associated with kidney problems.

Questions

You are responding to a 1-year-old who is reportedly seizing. The most common cause of seizures in children 6 months to 3 years old is

(A) fever.

(B) hypoxia.

(C) head injury.

(D) neurological deficit.

Your Answer _____

_____

Correct Answers

A–65

(A) The most common cause of seizures in patients 6 months to 3 years old is fever. Seizures may also occur as a result of a head injury. However, the question asks for the most common cause, which is a fever. These patients typically spike a high temperature and begin seizing. These types of seizures are called febrile seizures.

Questions

You are treating a patient with a history of seizures. The patient tells you that she is getting a strange smelling sensation. Within a few seconds the patient begins seizing. The period prior to the seizure when the patient experienced a strange odor is referred to as

(A) the tonic phase.

(B) the postictal phase.

(C) the clonic phase.

(D) an aura.

Your Answer _____

Fast Fact

The mission of the National Association of Emergency Medical Technicians is to represent and serve Emergency Medical Services personnel through advocacy, educational programs and research. Visit them online at www.naemt.org to learn more.

Correct Answers

A–66

(D) A seizure patient may experience a sensation prior to seizing in the form of a strange taste, odor, sound, or visual disturbance. This is called an aura. Most seizure patients recognize this phase and know they will begin seizing.

Questions

The patient in the previous question has stopped seizing. She is now in a gradual state of awakening. This phase of a seizure is called

(A) the tonic phase.

(B) the postictal phase.

(C) the clonic phase.

(D) an aura.

Your Answer _____

A patient who is suffering a severe allergic reaction is said to be suffering from

(A) asthma.

(B) syncope.

(C) anaphylactic shock.

(D) hayfever.

Your Answer _____

Correct Answers

A–67

(B) The phase immediately following a seizure until the patient becomes awake and alert is called the postictal phase. This phase may take up to 30 minutes. During this phase the EMT-B should concentrate on protecting the patient's airway and monitoring the patient.

A–68

(C) A patient who is suffering from a severe allergic reaction is referred to as having anaphylactic shock. In anaphylactic shock, the patient's whole body is affected. This is considered a life-threatening condition and immediate care is needed. If the patient has an Epi pen, you need to contact medical control, and then assist administering the injection after medical control approves.

Questions

Q–69

The most serious side effect of alcohol consumption is

(A) liver damage.

(B) hepatitis.

(C) death.

(D) loss of consciousness.

Your Answer _____

_____

Q–70

The only contraindication of administering the patient's epinephrine for an allergic reaction is

(A) There are no contraindications in this scenario.

(B) hypertension.

(C) hypotension.

(D) tachycardia.

Your Answer _____

_____

Correct Answers

A–69

(C) A patient may get any of the four items listed from alcohol; however, too much alcohol, like anything, may kill the patient.

A–70

(A) When a patient is experiencing anaphylactic shock or a severe allergic reaction, there are no contraindications in administering epinephrine. The patient may experience an increased heart rate and be very anxious. These are normal side effects of epinephrine. Anaphylactic shock is a true life-threatening emergency and must be treated as quickly as possible.

Questions

Which of the following list the routes by which a poison can enter the body?

(A) ingestion, inhalation, injection, and absorption

(B) injection, ingestion, and inhalation

(C) inhalation, abduction, injection, and ingestion

(D) inducement, absorption, indigestion, and inhalation

Your Answer _____

_____

Career Pulse

An EMT-1 has the emergency skills to assess a patient's condition and manage respiratory, cardiac, and trauma emergencies.

Correct Answers

A–71

(A) There are four ways a poison can enter the body. First is by swallowing or ingesting the poison. Second is by breathing the poison or inhalation. Third is by injection, and last is by absorption through the skin.

Questions

You are treating a patient with suspected poisoning. You are going to administer activated charcoal to the patient. The correct dose for the patient is

(A) 1 gram of activated charcoal for every year the patient is old.

(B) 1 gram of activated charcoal for every 1 pound of the patient's weight.

(C) 1 gram of activated charcoal for every 1 kilogram of the patient's weight.

(D) 1 gram of activated charcoal.

Your Answer _____

_____

Correct Answers

A–72

(C)   The correct dosage is one gram of activated charcoal for every one kilogram of the patient's body weight. If you know the patient's weight in pounds, the easiest way to convert pounds to kilograms is to divide by 2. Keep in mind that the exact conversion factor is 2.2 kilograms equals 1 pound. It is easier to divide by 2 however. If the patient weighed 200 pounds, then he would weigh 100 kilograms and the correct dosage would be 100 grams of activated charcoal.

Questions

You are treating a patient who has burns around the mouth. You note that the lips and the soft tissue around the mouth is swollen. The patient appears very anxious and in severe pain. The most likely cause of these symptoms is what type of poisoning?

(A) exposure to radiation

(B) inhaled gas

(C) medication reaction

(D) corrosive materials

Your Answer _____

_____

Correct Answers

(D) A patient who has ingested a corrosive substance will show with these signs and symptoms. Care must be taken not to cause the patient to vomit. If the substance burned and caused damage going in, it will cause damage coming back out.

Questions

$$\boxed{911}$$

You arrive on the scene to find an unresponsive female patient who is in her car in the garage. The car is still running and the door is closed. Looking through an outside window, your next action would be to

(A) attempt an immediate rescue.

(B) open the large garage door and any other outside openings.

(C) wait for the car to run out of gas.

(D) shut the car off immediately and remove the patient.

Your Answer _____

_____

Correct Answers

$$\boxed{911}$$

(B) The first priority is your safety. Do not attempt a rescue in an unsafe environment. The first step is to open the garage door and any other openings to the outside to get fresh air in the environment. An attempt to rescue should only be made after the scene becomes safe or there are appropriate PPE to make the rescue.

Questions

Q–75

911

The patient in the previous question is most likely suffering from

(A) diabetic coma.

(B) carbon monoxide poisoning.

(C) suicide attempt.

(D) heart attack.

Your Answer _____

Q–76

911

You would expect the patient in the previous question to have what type of appearance?

(A) cherry red

(B) pale

(C) cyanotic

(D) ashen/gray

Your Answer _____

Correct Answers

A-75

911

(B) Any of these answers could be true. However, it is safe to assume that this patient is suffering from carbon monoxide poisoning as a result of the vehicle running in an enclosed environment without adequate ventilation.

A-76

911

(A) A patient who is suffering from carbon monoxide poisoning is said to have a cherry red color appearance.

Questions

911

A patient at a fertilizer plant has a white powder over his arms. He is feeling ill and complaining of dizziness. The patient tells you he has been working in the fertilizer shed all day and a few of the bags broke open, spilling onto him. You remove the patient from the environment. Your next step would be to

(A) brush all the loose powder off the patient.

(B) begin flushing the patient with water.

(C) immediately transport the patient to the nearest hospital.

(D) wait for the haz mat team to arrive.

Your Answer _____

_____

Fast Fact

In 1969, President Lyndon Johnson's Committee on Highway Traffic Safety recommended the creation of a national certification agency to establish uniform standards for training and examination of personnel active in the delivery of emergency ambulance service. The result of this recommendation was the inception of the National Registry of Emergency Medical Technicians (NREMT) in 1970. To learn more about them, visit www.nremt.org.

Correct Answers

911

(A) A patient who has dry powder on them should have as much of the powder brushed off of them as possible. After this has been done, you would then flush the area with large amounts of water. Some chemicals react with water and you want as little contaminant on the patient as possible. Since the patient is not in an environment that will harm you and the patient knows what the substance is, it typically is not necessary to wait on the haz mat team before you begin to decontaminate. Care should be taken to avoid contaminating you or other persons. You always want to decontaminate prior to transporting a patient.

Questions

911

A patient had hydrochloric acid splash in her eyes. You find the patient at the eye wash station. Her supervisor tells you she has been flushing her eyes for five minutes. You should

(A) have the patient stop flushing and examine the eyes.

(B) have the patient stop flushing her eyes and bandage both eyes.

(C) have the patient continue flushing for at least another 15 minutes.

(D) immediately transport the patient to the hospital.

Your Answer _____

_____

Correct Answers

911

(C)   Any patient that has a chemical on their skin or in their eyes should flush the affected area for at least twenty minutes. This patient has been flushing her eyes for 5 minutes; therefore she should continue to flush her eyes for an additional 15 minutes. En route to the hospital, you should still continue to flush the eyes to help relieve the pain and remove any remaining chemical.

Questions

You are dispatched to the local high school for a 16-year-old football player who appears very excited. The patient has a pulse of 130, and a respiratory rate of 28. The patient states that he has not slept for the past two days. The patient's blood pressure is 180/110. The patient denies taking any medications, but is concerned about his weight. You would suspect this patient may have overdosed on

(A) codeine.

(B) LSD.

(C) methadone.

(D) ephedrine.

Your Answer _____

_____

Correct Answers

(D) These signs and symptoms are indicative of a stimulant overdose. Ephedrine is a stimulant and may cause all of these signs and symptoms. Some individuals may naturally react to a drug without taking an overdose. The patient may not be able to tolerate the recommended dose of the drug or medication.

Questions

A 29-year-old male has taken LSD. The patient appears very anxious and in a panic state. He is showing signs of paranoia. You should

(A) agree with everything the patient says.

(B) restrain the patient.

(C) be aggressive and talk very straight and stern to the patient.

(D) talk the patient down by reassuring the patient.

Your Answer _____

_____

Correct Answers

A–80

(D) It is important to talk a patient down when they have taken a hallucinogenic drug. Make the patient feel welcome. Be sure to identify yourself. It is important to let them know you are there to help them. Reassure the patient that the drug reaction will not last forever. Keep orienting the patient to place and time. You will also want to warn the patient of how they will feel when the drug begins to wear off. After you get the patient calmed down, transport them to the hospital.

Questions

$$\boxed{911}$$

Your patient was playing softball and was struck in the abdomen with a line drive. She is complaining of pain in the upper right quadrant of the abdomen. Which of the following organs would you suspect may be injured?

(A) the liver

(B) the spleen

(C) the right kidney

(D) the right lung

Your Answer _____

Correct Answers

$$\boxed{911}$$

(A) The liver is located in the right upper quadrant of the abdomen and is the most likely organ that would be injured by a direct blow to this quadrant. The spleen is located in the left upper quadrant. The kidney is located in the retro-peritoneal area and would be considered if she was struck in the lower right side of the back or possibly in the right flank area. The right lung may be injured, but typically the patient would have had a blow to the chest versus the abdomen. Thus, the liver is the best answer for this question.

Questions

911

There are hollow and solid organs in the abdomen. The gall bladder is considered a hollow organ. A ruptured hollow organ such as the gall bladder is most commonly associated with

(A) severe bleeding.

(B) inflammation and infection.

(C) gall stones.

(D) appendicitis.

Your Answer _____

Career Pulse

An EMT-Intermediate (EMT-2 and EMT-3) has more advanced training that allows the administration of intravenous fluids, the use of manual defibrillators, and the application of advanced airway techniques and equipment.

Correct Answers

$$\boxed{911}$$

(B) Infection and inflammation is most commonly associated with hollow organs. Severe bleeding is most commonly associated with solid organs.

Questions

You are treating a fifty-year-old female. She is complaining of nausea and vomiting. She has abdominal tenderness and distention. She states that her pain radiates from the navel to the back and shoulders. Her pulse is rapid and she is warm to the touch. You would suspect this patient is suffering from

(A) pancreatitis.

(B) esophageal varices.

(C) abdominal aortic aneurysm.

(D) appendicitis.

Your Answer _____

_____

Correct Answers

(A)   These signs and symptoms are typical of pancreatitis. Appendicitis typically presents with pain in the right lower quadrant. A patient with appendicitis will have a low-grade fever, chills, loss of appetite, and abdominal guarding. Patients with abdominal aortic aneurysms typically complain of a sudden onset of severe, constant abdominal pain. They may be nauseated and vomiting. The abdomen may be mottled and the lower extremities may be pale due to decreased blood supply. You may feel a pulsating mass in the abdomen around the umbilicus.

Questions

Your patient is vomiting large amounts of bright red blood. The patient does not complain of any pain or tenderness in the abdomen during your assessment. The patient's pulse is 128 and he is having difficulty breathing. His skin is pale, cool, and clammy. You notice he has a jaundiced appearance. You would suspect this patient has

(A) pancreatitis.

(B) esophageal varices.

(C) abdominal aortic aneurysm.

(D) appendicitis.

Your Answer _____

Correct Answers

A–84

(B) These signs and symptoms are indicative of esophageal varices. It is important to be prepared to suction this patient's airway to remove any blood.

Questions

Q–85

The process of losing heat through direct contact is called

(A) radiation.

(B) convection.

(C) conduction.

(D) evaporation.

Your Answer _____

Q–86

The process of losing heat through air movement is called

(A) radiation.

(B) convection.

(C) conduction.

(D) evaporation.

Your Answer _____

Correct Answers

A–85

(C) The transfer of heat from surface to another surface is called radiation. The process of losing heat through direct contact is conduction.

A–86

(B) The process of transferring heat through the air is convection. Evaporation is when a liquid changes to a vapor.

Questions

You are treating an alert, responsive patient suffering from hypothermia. Your first priority in caring for this patient is

(A) airway maintenance.

(B) removing the patient from the cold and preventing further heat loss.

(C) determining the patient's temperature.

(D) immediately transporting the patient.

Your Answer _____

_____

Fast Fact

*EMS care may be provided by the
fire department, an ambulance service, a county-
or government-based service, a hospital, or by a
combination of the above.*

Correct Answers

A–87

(B) The hypothermic patient is one of the few patients where airway control is not the first step in the patient care algorithm. You want to immediately remove the patient from the cold environment and prevent further heat loss. Removing any wet clothing and drying the patient is important. Then begin the re-warming process.

Questions

The patient you are treating has white, waxy skin on both hands. The patient's hands feel as if they are frozen. They are swollen and you notice that blisters are forming. Which of the following would you NOT want to do in caring for this patient?

(A) rub the hands

(B) remove any jewelry

(C) cover the hands with dry sterile dressings

(D) leave blisters intact

Your Answer _____

_____

Correct Answers

A–88

(A) When caring for a patient with localized cold injuries, you want to carefully remove any jewelry or restrictive clothing. Cover the affected area with dry sterile dressings and avoid applying any pressure. Do not break the blisters and do not rub or massage the affected area. Also do not apply heat or re-warm the skin with these patients and avoid allowing the patient to use the affected part.

Questions

It is a very hot and humid day. You are on standby at the local high school football game. The coach summons you over to the bench to assess one of his players. The patient is a 17-year-old male complaining of a headache. The patient's breathing is shallow and weak, and his skin is hot and dry to the touch. He has been vomiting and is very weak. This patient appears to be suffering from

(A) heat cramps.

(B) heat exhaustion.

(C) heat stroke.

(D) dehydration.

Your Answer _____

_____

Correct Answers

A–89

(C)   The best answer for this question is heat stroke. The patient is also probably dehydrated. However this patient presents a dire emergency beyond just dehydration. Heat stroke is a life-threatening condition that needs immediate care. The clue to this condition is the fact that the patient's skin is hot and dry. Patients will be warm and diaphoretic in heat exhaustion, but when their skin becomes hot and dry, they need immediate care.

Questions

The treatment for the patient in the previous question would be to

(A) give the patient lots of fluids to drink.

(B) transport the patient immediately.

(C) assess the patient for other injuries.

(D) immediately cool the patient.

Your Answer _____

_____

Which of the following patient characteristics does NOT represent a potential for violence?

(A) quick irregular movements

(B) threatening posture

(C) large, muscular individual

(D) loud, thunderous voice

Your Answer _____

_____

Correct Answers

A–90

(D) A patient suffering from heat stroke should be removed from the environment and immediately cooled using ice packs. The ice packs should be placed in the groin area and under the patient's arms. The only thing that should take precedence over cooling the patient is ensuring the patient has an airway.

A–91

(C) Just because a patient is large and/or muscular does not make them a potentially violent patient. Common signs of a potentially violent patient include: nervous pacing, shouting, threatening, cursing, throwing objects, clenched teeth and/or fists.

Questions

911

You are examining a patient who has been working in her backyard. The patient tells you she was
cleaning out a drainage area when she felt a sharp
pain on the hand. On examination of the patient's
hand, you see two holes on one side of the hand
that resemble a snake bite. Your treatment for this
patient would include

(A) keeping the patient calm, removing any jewelry, and applying a constricting band.

(B) keeping the patient calm, removing any jewelry, and applying a cold pack to the bite.

(C) keeping the patient calm, applying a cold
pack to the bite, and applying a constricting
band.

(D) keeping the patient calm, removing any jewelry, making an "x" cut on the wounds, and
sucking the venom out.

Your Answer _____

_____

Correct Answers

$$\boxed{911}$$

(A)   There about 45,000 patients bitten by snakes each year in the United States. The majority of these are not venomous snakes. If you can identify the snake and/or safely kill the snake, take it to the emergency room for identification. Patients that are bitten by a snake should be kept calm. The affected part of the body should be kept lower than the heart. Using a constricting band between the bite and patient's heart is recommended. You should not apply ice nor should you try to lance the wound and suck the venom out. The patient needs to be transported to a local hospital where the anti-venom is available. It is always a good idea to contact the hospital prior to transport to ensure that they have the anti-venom.

Questions

911

A patient was stung by a stingray at the local beach. The patient is complaining of severe pain in the ankle where she was stung. The appropriate treatment for this patient is

(A) keeping the patient calm, removing any jewelry, and applying a constricting band.

(B) keeping the patient calm, removing the stinger, and applying heat.

(C) keeping the patient calm, removing the stinger, and applying an ice pack.

(D) keeping the patient calm, removing the embedded stinger, and applying an ice pack.

Your Answer _____

Correct Answers

$$\boxed{911}$$

(B) Patients that are stung by marine life are treated differently than most other stings and bites. If the stinger can be removed easily and is not embedded in the patient's skin, it should be removed. Any jewelry should be removed in case of swelling. Any marine life stings or bites should have heat applied to the wound. Most lifeguards will volunteer to urinate on the wound. The warmth of the urine plus the ammonia in the urine provides relief for the bite or sting. The EMT-B should not volunteer their urine relief services, but should remember that warm, not cold, is appropriate care for these patients.

Questions

911

A 22-year-old female was found floating in a pool. When you arrive, the patient is being held in a face-up position. The patient is unconscious, but is breathing and has a pulse. You should consider which of the following conditions during your treatment of this patient?

(A) possible aspiration of water

(B) possible neck injury

(C) hyperthermia

(D) none of the above

Your Answer _____

_____

Correct Answers

911

(B) Any patient that is found in a pool or other body of water should be suspected of having a cervical spine and/or head injury until proven otherwise. It is not common for patients to swallow water when they drown, at least in large quantities. Since this patient is breathing, she has an airway. It also is not common for patients to have hyperthermia; most patients will have hypothermia as a result of a near-drowning, but not hyperthermia. The only time this may be possible is if the patient had a near drowning event in a hot tub or similar circumstance. Near-drowning patients may also suffer from shock, soft tissue injury, spinal injuries, or internal or external bleeding. These patients should be treated as a trauma patient with a thorough assessment conducted.

Questions

911

You are called to assist a SCUBA diver who is having trouble breathing. The patient states that it started approximately 15 minutes after she surfaced. She complains of chest pain, dizziness, blurred vision, and nausea and vomiting. This patient is most likely suffering from

(A) pneumothorax.

(B) decompression sickness.

(C) barotrauma.

(D) an air embolism.

Your Answer _____

Career Pulse

EMT-Paramedics (EMT-4) provide the most extensive prehospital care. In addition to carrying out the procedures of EMTs-1, 2 and 3, paramedics may administer drugs orally and intravenously, interpret EKGs, perform endotracheal intubations, and use monitors and other complex equipment.

Correct Answers

(C) At this point the scene is safe and the patient does not appear to be a threat to anyone. Restraining him would not be appropriate. No matter how you may feel about what the patient is going to do, it is inappropriate for you to say that the patient is going to do something stupid. You should continue your treatment of the patient and not turn the scene over to law enforcement. It is appropriate to find out how the patient intended to kill himself. This will aid determining how to care for the patient.

Questions

$$\boxed{\textbf{911}}$$

You are called to assist a SCUBA diver who is having trouble breathing. The patient states that it started approximately 15 minutes after she surfaced. She complains of chest pain, dizziness, blurred vision, and nausea and vomiting. This patient is most likely suffering from

(A) pneumothorax.

(B) decompression sickness.

(C) barotrauma.

(D) an air embolism.

Your Answer _____

Career Pulse

EMT-Paramedics (EMT-4) provide the most extensive prehospital care. In addition to carrying out the procedures of EMTs-1, 2 and 3, paramedics may administer drugs orally and intravenously, interpret EKGs, perform endotracheal intubations, and use monitors and other complex equipment.

Correct Answers

A–95

$$\boxed{911}$$

(D)   Any of these could be associated with dive incidents, but these signs and symptoms are indicative of an air embolism. Divers who suffer from decompression sickness, or the bends, typically do not develop signs and symptoms of the bends for 12 to 24 hours after their dive. Barotrauma usually occurs as the diver is ascending or descending.

Correct Answers

(C) At this point the scene is safe and the patient does not appear to be a threat to anyone. Restraining him would not be appropriate. No matter how you may feel about what the patient is going to do, it is inappropriate for you to say that the patient is going to do something stupid. You should continue your treatment of the patient and not turn the scene over to law enforcement. It is appropriate to find out how the patient intended to kill himself. This will aid determining how to care for the patient.

Questions

You are called to the home of a 20-year-old male who is depressed. The patient states he is going to kill himself. Your first step in treating this patient after the scene is safe is to

(A) restrain the patient to prevent him from hurting himself.

(B) ask the patient why he wants to do something so stupid.

(C) ask the patient how he plans to kill himself.

(D) turn the scene over to law enforcement.

Your Answer _____

_____

Questions

There are three stages of labor. In the second stage of labor,

(A) labor pains develop.

(B) the cervix becomes dilated.

(C) the baby is born.

(D) the placenta is expelled.

Your Answer _____

911

Which of the following injuries is a true orthopedic emergency?

(A) fractured femur

(B) dislocated shoulder

(C) dislocated knee

(D) dislocated hip

Your Answer _____

Correct Answers

A–97

(C) In the first stage of labor, the cervix becomes fully dilated. During the second stage of labor, the infant moves through the birth canal and is born. During the third stage of labor, the placenta separates from the uterine wall and is expelled from the uterus.

A–98

(C) A dislocated knee is considered a true orthopedic emergency.

Questions

Any female of child-bearing age, 12 to 50 years old, who is complaining of abdominal pain, may be

(A) pregnant.

(B) suffering from influenza.

(C) having an appendicitis attack.

(D) having a severe reaction.

Your Answer _____

_____

Correct Answers

A–99

(A) Any female patient who is of child-bearing age from 12 to 50, may be pregnant if they are complaining of abdominal pain. This does not mean that a patient of this age range is pregnant just because she is having abdominal pain, but you should have a high suspicion. Even if she is taking birth control measures, the only foolproof way not to get pregnant is not to have sex. Consider questioning younger patients in private rather than having their parents present. They may deny having sex when questioned in front of their parents, so be cautious when asking questions in these circumstances.

Questions

You are called to the scene of a 23-year-old female patient who is complaining of a severe, persistent headache. She has been vomiting and complaining of abdominal pain. She states she has gained 5 pounds in the past week and thinks she may be pregnant. She has not been eating well and has not been urinating as often as usual. Upon physical exam her blood pressure is 170/102, pulse is 98, and respirations are 20. You would suspect this patient to be suffering from

(A) abruptio placenta.

(B) toxemia.

(C) gestation diabetes.

(D) ectopic pregnancy.

Your Answer _____

Correct Answers

(B) These are classic signs of the first stage of toxemia, which is called pre-eclampsia. In the second stage of toxemia, the patient experiences life-threatening seizures. During these seizures the placenta can separate from the uterine wall. Depending on the severity of the seizure, the patient and/or the fetus may die as a result of cerebral hemorrhage, respiratory arrest, kidney failure or circulatory collapse.

Questions

Q-101

The greatest and most frequent concern for the patient in the previous question is

(A) seizures.

(B) bleeding.

(C) miscarriage.

(D) imminent death.

Your Answer _____

_____

Q-102

A minute after the baby is born, the heart rate is less than 60 beats per minute. You should

(A) blow by oxygen.

(B) attempt to stimulate the newborn.

(C) aggressively warm the newborn.

(D) begin chest compressions.

Your Answer _____

_____

Correct Answers

A–101

(A)   As noted in the previous question, the most common and greatest concern for this patient is seizures.

A–102

(D)   Once the infant is born and the heart rate is below 100 beats per minute, is cyanotic and is not breathing adequately, you should begin ventilation assistance by bag-valve-mask at a rate of 40-60 ventilations per minute. If the infant doesn't improve with a heart rate of greater than 80 beats per minute after one minute of assisting ventilations, you should begin chest compressions.

Questions

Q–103

Which of the following is NOT an imminent sign that birthing is going to occur?

(A) Crowning has occurred.

(B) Contractions are 5 minutes apart.

(C) The patient feels the infant's head moving down the birth canal.

(D) The patient's abdomen is very hard.

Your Answer _____

_____

Q–104

When you examine your patient, you find that the baby is crowning. You prepare for an immediate birth. Once the head is out, the next step is to

(A) pull the rest of the baby out.

(B) suction the mouth first, then the nose.

(C) suction the nose, then the mouth.

(D) cut the umbilical cord.

Your Answer _____

_____

Correct Answers

A–103

(B) Contractions are typically closer than 2 minutes apart, are intense and last from 30 to 90 seconds. Delivery can be expected within the next few minutes if these signs and symptoms are present. The EMT-B should make preparations to deliver the baby.

A–104

(B) Once the baby's head is out, the next step would be to suction the mouth first then the nose. You want to suction the mouth first to avoid stimulating the baby and having it aspirate any fluid still in the mouth or pharynx. You never want to pull the baby out, but gently assist the birth of the baby.

Questions

911

Your patient is bleeding from the right arm. The blood is spurting and is bright red. The patient has most likely lacerated her

(A) vein.

(B) capillaries.

(C) artery.

(D) mesentery.

Your Answer _____

911

You continually apply bandages to the patient's arm in the previous question and it continues to soak through. Your next step is to

(A) apply a tourniquet.

(B) remove old bandages and apply new bandages.

(C) apply pressure at the pressure point.

(D) elevate the arm.

Your Answer _____

Correct Answers

A-105

$$\boxed{911}$$

(C) Arterial blood is typically bright red in color since it is oxygenated. Bleeding from an artery will typically spurt. Blood from a vein is typically dark red because it is unoxygenated and flows freely. Capillaries have dark red blood and it oozes. Blood exchanges oxygen at the capillary level.

A-106

$$\boxed{911}$$

(D) If the bleeding continues after applying direct pressure with a gauze pad, you should next elevate the arm to try to control the bleeding. After you have done both of these steps your next step would be to apply pressure at the pressure point. The last resort is the tourniquet and should virtually never be used.

Questions

911

The patient is bleeding severely from the lower leg. You have applied direct pressure and elevated the leg. Your next step is to apply pressure at the pressure point. The pressure point for this injury would be

(A) the popliteal artery.

(B) the femoral artery.

(C) the tibial artery.

(D) the dorsalis pedis artery.

Your Answer _____

◀ Fast Fact

The National Association of Emergency Medical Technicians represents EMTs from all types of services, (private, fire, volunteer, rural, urban, men and women) whereas other organizations may represent EMTs in certain areas. These groups include the International Association of Fire Fighters, the International Rescue and Emergency Care Association, and the National Volunteer Fire Council.

Correct Answers

$$\boxed{911}$$

(B) When applying pressure to a pressure point, you want to locate the artery pressure point proximal to the wound. In this case the femoral artery pressure point would be the most appropriate. The tibial artery is not considered a pressure point and is located below the injury as is the dorsalis pedis. The popliteal artery is also not a pressure point. Therefore the only option would be the femoral artery pressure point.

Questions

$\boxed{911}$

The appropriate care for a patient with Epistaxis is to

(A) have the patient lay down and remain calm.

(B) pinch the nostrils and have the patient lean forward.

(C) pinch the nostrils and have the patient lean back.

(D) have the patient lay in a supine position with his head lower than his body.

Your Answer _____

_____

Career Pulse
The most advanced level of training for this occupation is EMT-Paramedic.

Correct Answers

911

(B) Epistaxis is a nose bleed. In these cases you should have the patient pinch their nose and lean forward. You want to keep the patient in a sitting position and keep the patient calm. You don't want the patient to lean back and have the blood collect in the oropharnyx. This may cause the patient to choke on the blood, plus you do not want the patient to swallow blood which may make them nauseated and begin to vomit.

Questions

911

Your patient is complaining of abdominal pain. He tells you that his stools have been dark and tarry. His abdomen is tender upon palpation. You would suspect this patient is suffering from

(A) upper abdominal internal bleeding.

(B) lower abdominal internal bleeding.

(C) abdominal evisceration.

(D) bleeding from the colon.

Your Answer _____

Correct Answers

A–109

$$\boxed{911}$$

(A) You would suspect that this patient is having internal bleeding in the upper regions of the abdomen. Typically bright colored blood in the stool is indicative of a lower GI bleed and dark colored blood is indicative of upper GI bleed. An abdominal evisceration is when the patient's organs are protruding as a result of a traumatic event.

Questions

$\boxed{911}$

Which of the following are the signs and symptoms of shock in the early stages?

(A) tachycardia, anxious, restless, skin pale, cool, and clammy

(B) bradycardia, anxious, restless, skin pale, cool, and clammy

(C) tachycardia, hypotension, increased breathing

(D) bradycardia, hypotension, skin pale, cool and clammy

Your Answer _____

_____

Fast Fact

Every year, more than 600,000 Americans die from heart disease such as heart attacks and strokes. Heart disease is the leading cause of death among Americans.

Correct Answers

911

(A)   Early signs of shock include an increased heart rate, increased respirations, and pale, cool, clammy skin. The patient will be restless and anxious due to hypoxia. The patient also may have an altered mental status and pupils will dilate. It is important to note that once the blood pressure drops, you are in the late stages of shock. Hypotension is a late sign of shock.

Questions

911

You are treating a patient that has been involved in a motor vehicle accident. You can lift a flap of skin on the patient's head. This type of injury would be referred to as a(n)

(A) avulsion.

(B) laceration.

(C) evisceration.

(D) puncture.

Your Answer _____

_____

Correct Answers

A–111

911

(A) A puncture is created by an object that is typically sharp and pointed. A laceration is defined as a jagged cut. An evisceration is typically referred to as organs protruding. This injury would be referred to as an avulsion, which is a flap of skin.

Questions

911

Which of the following is NOT true of the treatment of an impaled object?

(A) remove if blocking the airway

(B) stabilize in place

(C) remove to accommodate transport of the patient

(D) control the bleeding

Your Answer _____

_____

Career Pulse

An EMT-Paramedic receives additional training in body function and learns more advanced skills.

Correct Answers

A–112

$$\boxed{911}$$

(C) The treatment of a patient with an impaled object includes: securing the object in place, exposing the wound area, controlling the bleeding, and using a bulky dressing to help stabilize the object. The only time it is permissible to remove an impaled object is if it is impeding the breathing of the patient.

Questions

911

The two major goals of treating a large open neck injury are

(A) bleeding control.

(B) air embolism prevention.

(C) A and B.

(D) neither A nor B.

Your Answer _____

_____

Correct Answers

A–113

$$\boxed{911}$$

(C) The two main concerns when treating large open neck wounds are controlling bleeding and the prevention of an air embolism. To treat these patients, place a gloved hand over the wound to control bleeding. Apply an occlusive dressing and cover the dressing with a regular dressing, applying only enough pressure to control the bleeding. Once the bleeding is controlled, apply a pressure dressing and treat for other injuries, including possible c-spine injuries.

Questions

$$\boxed{911}$$

A 35-year-old male was cutting wood. The saw slipped and cut three of his fingers off. Treat the patient by

(A) packing the amputated part in ice.

(B) placing the amputated part in cold sterile water.

(C) wrapping the amputated part in a dry sterile dressing and place on ice.

(D) wrapping the amputated part in a dry sterile dressing and keep the part cool.

Your Answer _____

_____

Fast Fact

More than 90,000 Americans die from accidents each year.

Correct Answers

$$\boxed{911}$$

(D) Amputated body parts should be wrapped in dry sterile dressings and placed in a plastic bag. The parts should be kept cool, but should never be placed directly on ice. The amputated parts should be transported with the patient to the hospital. If the parts are not found prior to transport, someone on the scene should continue to look for the parts, but transport should not be delayed. The amputated parts should be transported to the hospital once they are found.

Questions

911

The patient you are treating has blisters and intense pain over his hand. You find out from the patient's mother that the patient touched the burner of the stove. You would recognize this type of burn as a

(A) superficial burn.

(B) partial thickness burn.

(C) full thickness burn.

(D) complete thickness burn.

Your Answer _____

Correct Answers

911

(B) Superficial burns are red and painful at the site. Partial thickness burns have blisters, intense pain, the skin is white to red and is moist and mottled. Full thickness burns are charred, dark brown or white. The skin is hard to the touch and the patient has little to no pain since the nerve endings have been damaged. The patient will have pain around the periphery of the burn.

Questions

$$\boxed{911}$$

Which of the following injuries would be classified as belonging to a critical burn patient?

(A) any full thickness burn

(B) any burn to the arms or legs

(C) any partial thickness burn covering 15% or more body surface area

(D) full or partial thickness burn of the hands or feet

Your Answer _____

_____

Career Pulse

The Technology program for an EMT-Paramedic usually lasts up to 2 years and results in an associate degree in applied science. Such education prepares the graduate to take the NREMT examination and become certified as an EMT-Paramedic.

Correct Answers

911

(D) Any burns that involve the respiratory tract; full or partial thickness burns involving the face, hands, feet, genitalia, or respiratory tract; any full thickness burn covering 10% of body surface area or more; any partial thickness burn covering 20% or more body surface area; burn injuries complicated by a suspected fracture to an extremity; patients 55 years of age or older that have a moderate classified burn; and any burn that encircles a body part is classified as a critical burn.

Questions

911

The most important element at the scene of a patient that has burns from an electrical source is

(A) scene safety.

(B) airway control.

(C) cool the burn.

(D) check for an exit wound.

Your Answer _____

_____

Correct Answers

$$\boxed{911}$$

(A)   The most important aspect at the scene of an electrical injury is scene safety. After the scene is secured and the power has been turned off by the power company, the patient's airway is the next important aspect. Since electrical injuries usually cause an entrance and exit wound, it is important to check for the exit wound. Electricity takes the path of least resistance. Remember scene safety first, before attempting to treat the patient.

Questions

Q–118

Which of the following is not a function of the musculoskeletal system?

(A) gives the body shape

(B) protects internal organs

(C) provides for movement

(D) produces calcium

Your Answer _____

Q–119

Ligaments connect

(A) muscle to bone.

(B) bone to tendons.

(C) bone to bone.

(D) muscle to tendons.

Your Answer _____

Correct Answers

A–118

(D)   The three functions of the musculoskeletal system are to give the body shape, protect the internal organs and provide for movement.

A–119

(C)   Tendons connect muscle to bone. Ligaments connect bone to bone.

Questions

$$\boxed{911}$$

You just completed splinting a patient's fractured arm. Prior to applying the splint the patient had a distal pulse in the extremity. After splinting, you cannot find a radial pulse. You suspect that

(A) the fracture has cut off the circulation.

(B) your splint is too tight.

(C) this is a normal reaction after splinting.

(D) the patient's condition is worsening.

Your Answer _____

_____

More than 4 million babies are born in the U.S. each year.

Correct Answers

911

(B) The patient's condition is worsening, but is probably a direct result of you applying the splint too tightly. Loosen the splint and reassess for distal pulses. In most cases this will resolve the issue and the distal pulses will return. It is always important to check distal pulses prior to and after splinting. It is also a good idea to check motor and sensation along with capillary refill when you check for pulses.

Questions

911

Your patient has what appears to be a dislocated shoulder. Treatment for this patient should be to

(A) sling and swathe the injured shoulder.

(B) immobilize the arm to the side of the patient.

(C) reset the shoulder and then immobilize.

(D) wrap the upper body in a pillow and immobilize both arms.

Your Answer _____

_____

Correct Answers

911

(A) The appropriate treatment for a patient with a dislocated shoulder is to sling and swathe. Under no circumstances should an EMT-B attempt to reset a dislocated shoulder.

Questions

911

You are assessing a 24-year-old male who was involved in a bar room brawl. Witnesses say the patient was struck with a barstool. The patient is unresponsive. You note battle signs on your assessment. This is a sign of

(A) intracranial bleeding.

(B) basilar skull fracture.

(C) epidural hematoma.

(D) subdural hematoma.

Your Answer _____

Career Pulse

Extensive related coursework and clinical and field experience is required for an EMT-Paramedic certification.

Correct Answers

$$\boxed{911}$$

(B) Without further diagnostic exam you cannot rule out any of these possibilities. However, battle signs are indicative of a basilar skull fracture. Battle signs may appear thirty minutes to twelve hours after the initial injury. Raccoon eyes are usually indicative of intracranial bleeding.

Questions

911

A witness tells you that a patient became unresponsive immediately after being struck by a baseball, but then regained consciousness. The witness also tells you that the patient was complaining of a severe headache during the time she was conscious. The patient is now unresponsive. The right pupil is fixed and dilated. The bystander tells you the patient was struck on the right side of the head. The patient is most likely suffering from

(A) intracranial bleeding.

(B) a basilar skull fracture.

(C) a subdural hematoma.

(D) an epidural hematoma.

Your Answer _____

_____

Correct Answers

911

(D) These are classic signs of an epidural hematoma. You need to prepare for seizures. Patients who have an epidural hematoma commonly seize. Patients who have subdural hematomas, present with a deterioration in level of consciousness, dilation of one pupil, abnormal respirations, rising blood pressure, and slowing pulse.

Questions

Which of the following influences the activities of involuntary muscles and glands including the heart?

(A) central nervous system

(B) peripheral nervous system

(C) voluntary nervous system

(D) autonomic nervous system

Your Answer _____

911

When treating an eye injury involving an impaled object, it is important to

(A) cover both eyes and stabilize the object.

(B) cover the affected eye and stabilize the object.

(C) stabilize the object and do not cover either eye.

(D) remove the object and cover both eyes.

Your Answer _____

Correct Answers

A–124

(D) The central nervous system refers to the brain and the spinal cord. The peripheral nervous system consists of nerves located outside of the brain and the spinal cord. The voluntary nervous system influences activities of voluntary muscles and movements throughout the body. The autonomic nervous system is therefore what is described in this question.

A–125

(A) Eyes have sympathetic movement, which means if one eye moves, the other eye moves. Therefore, any time you have an eye injury and you do not want the patient to move their eye, such as a patient with an impaled object in the eye, it is important to not only stabilize the impaled object, but also to cover both eyes.

Questions

911

Your patient is complaining of not being able to feel anything and cannot move any of his extremities. He fails your PMS test and you notice that he has diaphragmatic breathing. You suspect this patient has a spinal cord injury

(A) in the cervical spine region.

(B) in the thoracic spine region.

(C) in the lumbar spine region.

(D) in the sacral spine region.

Your Answer _____

_____

◄ Fast Fact

Each year, 800,000 Americans seek medical attention for dog bites; half of these are children. Of those injured, 386,000 require treatment in an emergency department and about a dozen die.
[http://www.cdc.gov/ncipc/duip/biteprevention.htm]

Correct Answers

911

(A) Patients with these complaints typically have a spinal cord injury in the neck region. If the patient has the same signs and symptoms but can feel, wave, and squeeze his hands, then the injury is typically below the neck. If the patient has normal breathing, can feel, wave and squeeze their hands, but cannot feel, wiggle or raise their toes and feet, then it typically indicates a lower spinal cord injury.

Questions

$$\boxed{911}$$

You should remove the helmet from a patient in all of the following scenarios EXCEPT:

(A) The helmet does not interfere with your ability to assess and reassess airway and breathing.

(B) The helmet interferes with your ability to assess or reassess airway and breathing.

(C) The helmet interferes with your ability to adequately manage the airway or breathing.

(D) The helmet does not fit well and allows excessive movement of the head inside the helmet.

Your Answer _____

_____

Correct Answers

$$\boxed{911}$$

(A) You should also remove the helmet if it interferes with proper spinal immobilization or the patient is in cardiac arrest.

Questions

911

You are treating a patient who has a possible spinal injury after falling approximately 12 feet. The patient is warm and dry. The patient's vital signs are pulse 80, respirations 20, and BP 118/76. When you reassess the patient's vital signs 5 minutes later, the pulse and respirations are the same, but the BP has dropped to 80/40. You would suspect this patient is suffering from

(A) cardiogenic shock.

(B) vasogenic shock.

(C) neurogenic shock.

(D) hypovolemic shock.

Your Answer _____

_____

Correct Answers

911

(C)   Patients who have a spinal injury may suddenly drop their blood pressure although their vital signs, skin color and temperature remain the same. This is a result of the arteries losing the nerve impulse from the brain and the spinal cord as a result of the injury. This is typically indicative when the patient has injured the upper portion of their spinal cord. This is called relative hypovolemia. The patient's pump, the heart, is intact and functioning properly. The patient's blood volume has not increased, however, their pipes, the blood vessels, have increased or dilated in size. You have the same amount or volume of blood, but now a larger pipe or vessel for the same amount of blood to go through, therefore decreasing the pressure against the arterial walls and dropping the blood pressure.

Questions

When decontaminating a patient's eye that has a foreign body or substance in it, you should always

(A) have the patient close their unaffected eye and flush the area with water.

(B) wash the eye towards the nose so you can watch the substance dislodge from the eye.

(C) lay the patient on his back and flush with copious amounts of water.

(D) flush the affected eye, flushing away from the unaffected eye with copious amounts of water.

Your Answer _____

_____

Career Pulse

Due to the longer training requirement, almost all EMT-Paramedics are in paid positions, rather than being volunteers.

Correct Answers

A-129

(D) You should always flush the affected eye away from the unaffected eye. Have the patient lie on the side of their affected eye and flush the eye by holding the eyelid open and flush continuously for at least 15 minutes. You never want to flush towards the unaffected eye, because you will flush the contaminants or particles into the unaffected eye.

Questions

911

A 20-year-old female patient was sexually assaulted. The patient states that she is hemorrhaging profusely from the vagina. You should

(A) do nothing, and transport immediately.

(B) apply a sterile sanitary napkin.

(C) pack the vagina with sterile dressings.

(D) have the patient squeeze her legs together and transport immediately.

Your Answer _____

_____

Correct Answers

$$\boxed{911}$$

(B) Dealing with these types of events is not easy. The EMT-B needs to be very sensitive to the patient's experience while treating the patient with the appropriate medical care. In this instance you would want to apply a sanitary napkin and apply direct pressure to control the bleeding. You never want to insert or pack anything into the vagina. It is important to have a female EMT-B assist the patient if at all possible.

Questions

A 45-year-old male was involved in an MVA. The patient is complaining of shortness of breath and chest pain. You recognize that the patient has JVD and the patient's pulse is weak and thready. You believe the patient has a pericardial tamponade. You distinguish that this is the problem with the patient by noting or discovering

(A) decreased heart sounds.

(B) patient has JVD.

(C) narrowing pulse pressure.

(D) patient is complaining of chest pain.

Your Answer _____

_____

Fast Fact

In 2000, 160 children ages 14 years or younger died from an obstruction of the respiratory tract due to inhaled or ingested foreign bodies. Of these, 41% were caused by food items and 59% by nonfood objects. [http://www.cdc.gov/ncipc/duip/spotlite/choking.htm]

Correct Answers

A–131

(C) All of these are signs and symptoms of a pericardial tamponade. A narrowing pulse pressure is indicative of a pericardial tamponade. A narrowing pulse pressure is when the systolic and diastolic grow closer together. Decreased heart sounds may also be a sign, but it is not always indicative of a pericardial tamponade. This may also be a result of a pneumothorax or hemothorax.

Questions

911

You are dispatched to a local farm. You arrive on the scene to discover that the patient is inside a silo. The patient does not respond to your verbal commands from outside the silo. You should

(A) immediately rescue the patient.

(B) enter the silo, with your partner waiting outside.

(C) wear an SCBA and enter.

(D) empty the contents of the silo.

Your Answer _____

_____

Correct Answers

$$\boxed{911}$$

(C) The main concern with a silo is the gas that it produces. If one person is already unresponsive in a confined space such as a silo, anyone else who enters will typically be overcome by the same gases. Remember, scene safety and wearing protective equipment is important. It is also important to only use equipment you have been properly trained to use.

Questions

When treating children, all of the following are important considerations EXCEPT

(A) the fact that they are more susceptible to hypothermia.

(B) that padding is needed when immobilizing.

(C) that they should be treated just like adults.

(D) that they have smaller airways.

Your Answer _____

_____

Career Pulse

EMTs and paramedics held about 179,000 jobs in 2002.

Correct Answers

A–133

(C)   A child's skin surface is large compared to their body mass, which makes them more susceptible to hypothermia in cold environments. They also tend to have large heads compared to the rest of their body and tend to take more padding when immobilizing them on spine boards. Their airways are also smaller and more prone to choking or other airway problems as a result of swelling. A child's airway may be as small as ½ the size of a typical adult's trachea. Children are different from adults and must be treated like children.

Questions

Which of the following are signs of early respiratory distress in children?

(A) nasal flaring

(B) neck muscle retractions

(C) see-saw respirations

(D) all of the above

Your Answer _____

Correct Answers

(D) Signs of early respiratory distress in children are: increased respiratory rate, nasal flaring, intercostals retractions on inspiration, supraclavicular and subcostal retractions on inspirations, neck muscle retractions, audible breathing noises such as stridor, wheezing, or grunting, and see-saw respirations. It is important to identify respiratory distress in children and infants early. These patients tend to compensate for a period of time and then crash fast. Early intervention is important.

Questions

$$\boxed{911}$$

When establishing a landing zone for a medical helicopter, the minimum area secured should be

(A) 100' × 100'.

(B) 200' × 200'.

(C) 50' × 50'.

(D) 60' × 60'.

Your Answer _____

_____

Fast Fact

For every choking-related death, there are more than 100 visits to U.S. emergency departments. [http://www.cdc.gov/ncipc/duip/spotlite/choking.htm]

Correct Answers

911

(A) The minimum area you should secure for a night landing of a medical helicopter is 100' × 100'. During the daylight hours it is 60' × 60'. Keep in mind your local air medical agency may require a larger landing area depending on their policies and the type of helicopter they use.

Questions

911

A frantic mother hands you her 9-month-old infant. She says the patient was playing and found a marble. The patient stuck the marble in his mouth and she cannot get him to breathe. You should

(A) deliver 5 back blows followed by 5 chest compressions.

(B) deliver 5 back blows followed by 5 abdominal thrusts.

(C) sweep the mouth to see if you can feel the marble.

(D) deliver 5 abdominal thrusts.

Your Answer _____

_____

Correct Answers

A–136

$$\boxed{911}$$

(A)   When treating an infant who is choking, you should never stick your fingers in their mouth nor do a blind finger sweep. You should only do a finger sweep if you see the object. The proper treatment for a choking infant is to deliver 5 back blows, 5 chest thrusts and then look in the mouth for the object. If the patient is unresponsive then try a ventilation and proceed with the same sequence if you cannot get a ventilation into the patient.

Questions

A 4-year-old patient you are treating has a fever of 104° F. The patient tells his mother it hurts to swallow. You notice that he is drooling from his mouth and he appears to be mouth breathing. The patient wants to sit in a tripod position. You suspect the patient is suffering from

(A) croup.

(B) epiglottitis.

(C) asthma.

(D) bronchitis.

Your Answer _____

Career Pulse

Most career EMTs and paramedics work in metropolitan areas.

Correct Answers

(B)   The patient is exhibiting signs indicative of epiglottitis. It is important not to agitate this patient and get the patient to definitive care immediately. Try to provide oxygen to the patient, but do not agitate the child or stick anything in the patient's mouth in doing so.

Questions

911

Which of the following patient moving devices would be most appropriate to lift a patient with a dislocated hip from the floor in a narrow hallway?

(A) backboard

(B) bed sheet

(C) stair chair

(D) scoop stretcher

Your Answer _____

Correct Answers

911

(D)   The most appropriate device to lift a patient from the floor that has a dislocated hip and is lying in a narrow hallway is the scoop stretcher. The scoop stretcher can be split in half and slid under each side of the patient and then reconnected. It allows for minimal movement. The other devices would require additional movement of the patient and may aggravate the patient's injury.

Questions

You immobilized a 37-year-old pregnant female on a backboard. The patient states that she is feeling dizzy and weak. Her blood pressure has dropped and she is tachycardic. You should

(A) elevate the foot of the board 6 inches.

(B) apply the MAST garment and inflate the legs.

(C) raise the right side of the board 6 inches.

(D) raise the left side of the board 6 inches.

Your Answer _____

_____

Fast Fact

In 2001, an estimated 17,537 children 14 years or younger were treated in U.S. emergency departments for choking episodes. Coins were involved in 18% of all choking-related emergency department visits for children ages 1 to 4 years. [http://www.cdc.gov/ncipc/ duip/spotlite/choking.htm]

Correct Answers

A–139

(C) Pregnant patients, especially in their late terms, should be transported on their left side. By placing the patient in a supine position, the fetus will place pressure on the inferior vena cava causing the blood pressure to drop, cardiac output to decrease, and the pulse to increase. Raising the right side of the board 6 inches or more will help take the pressure off the patient's inferior vena cava.

Questions

You are working at a haz mat site. You should establish the medical care of all patients to be performed in the

(A) cold zone.

(B) warm zone.

(C) hot zone.

(D) none of the above

Your Answer _____

_____

Correct Answers

A–140

(A) With the exception of treating life-threatening care such as airway management and immobilization, all medical care should be performed in the cold zone. Without the proper personal protective equipment and training, an EMT-B should remain in the cold zone and treat the patients once they have been effectively decontaminated.

Questions

911

What three things do you want to remember when dealing with a radioactive incident?

(A) time, depth, and shielding

(B) time, distance, and shielding

(C) time, distance, and space

(D) type, distance, and shielding

Your Answer _____

_____

Career Pulse

After an ambulance run, EMTs and paramedics replace used supplies and check equipment.

Correct Answers

911

(B) The three most important factors when dealing with radioactive materials are time, distance, and shielding. Radioactive materials are classified into three categories: alpha, beta, and gamma. Gamma is the most intense radioactive material. The length of time you are exposed to gamma radiation cannot be long compared to time exposed to alpha rays. Exposure to alpha rays occurs almost daily from the sun's rays. Distance and protection or shielding from radioactive materials are also important factors. Alpha rays will not penetrate through paper while lead is needed to protect against gamma rays.

Questions

911

At the scene of a mass casualty incident, the _____ _____ is in charge of where the patient goes.

(A) EMT-B treating the patient

(B) transportation sector

(C) incident commander

(D) driver of the ambulance

Your Answer _____

_____

Correct Answers

$$\boxed{911}$$

(B) During a mass casualty incident, an incident command system needs to be established which includes a transportation sector. The responsibility of this sector is to ensure that patients are transported to the appropriate hospitals. The transportation sector coordinates this with the incident commander, the triage sector, and the hospitals, but is responsible for where the patient is transported to and then recording this information.

Questions

911

You are the triage officer at the scene of a mass casualty incident. Which of the following patients should be treated first?

(A) a 37-year-old female patient who is unresponsive

(B) an 18-year-old male patient who is not breathing and has no pulse

(C) a 29-year-old male patient with a femur fracture

(D) an 8-year-old patient who is conscious but having trouble breathing

Your Answer _____

_____

Fast Fact

In 2000, there were 3,281 unintentional drownings in the United States, averaging nine people per day. This does not include drownings in boating-related incidents. [http://www.cdc.gov/ncipc/factsheets/ drown.htm]

Correct Answers

$$\boxed{911}$$

(A) In a mass casualty incident, anyone who is pulseless and apneic is classified as dead. Unfortunately, often there are too many patients to care for considering the amount of resources available. A patient with a fractured femur will be stable for the moment. An 8-year-old with trouble breathing may be tagged as a moderate priority, but the unconscious female is a high priority and should be treated first. If the patient's airway can be opened with manual techniques, continue to triage and provide treatment to other patients.

Questions

The 2-person ratio of chest compressions to ventilations for an adult patient is

(A) 30:2.

(B) 4:1.

(C) 5:1.

(D) 15:2.

Your Answer _____

_____

The depth of compressions for a patient that is 6 years old is

(A) ½ to 1 inch.

(B) ⅓ to ½ the depth of the chest.

(C) ½ to ¾ the depth of the chest.

(D) 2 to 2 ½ inches.

Your Answer _____

_____

Correct Answers

A–144

(A) The ratio of compressions to breaths for adults is 30:2, regardless of whether you have one rescuer or two rescuers.

A–145

(B) The chest wall should be compressed ⅓ to ½ the depth of the chest.

Questions

911

You are treating a 35-year-old conscious choking victim. The patient suddenly goes unresponsive. Your next step is to

(A) attempt to ventilate the patient.

(B) perform CPR.

(C) deliver 5 abdominal thrusts.

(D) deliver 5 chest thrusts.

Your Answer _____

_____

Career Pulse

If a transported patient had a contagious disease, EMTs and paramedics decontaminate the interior of the ambulance and report cases to the proper authorities.

Correct Answers

$$\boxed{911}$$

(B) As a health care provider, once the patient becomes unresponsive you should begin CPR.

Questions

You have successfully converted your cardiac arrest patient out of v-fib with your AED. The patient has a pulse and respirations are 6 per minute. You should

(A) continue CPR.

(B) monitor the patient.

(C) administer 15 lpm of oxygen via NRB.

(D) continue to assist the patient with ventilations via a BVM and oxygen.

Your Answer _____

_____

Correct Answers

A-147

(D) Once you have converted a patient out of v-fib and the patient has a pulse, you can stop doing chest compressions. Since this patient only has a respiratory rate of 6 per minute, you would continue to assist ventilations until their respiratory rate is between 12-20 breaths per minute. At that time you would monitor the patient and continue to provide supplemental oxygen at a rate of 15 L/min via non-rebreather mask.

Questions

After arriving at the hospital you notice blood on your stretcher. The most appropriate way to disinfect the stretcher is a(n)

(A) 1:10 ratio of bleach to water solution.

(B) 1:100 ratio of bleach to water solution.

(C) 1:1000 ratio of bleach to water solution.

(D) straight bleach solution.

Your Answer _____

_____

Fast Fact

For every child who drowns, three receive emergency department care for non-fatal submersion injuries. More than 40% of these children require hospitalization. [http://www.cdc.gov/ncipc/factsheets/drown.htm]

Correct Answers

A–148

(A) Since the stretcher comes in direct contact with your skin, you want to use a 1:10 bleach to water solution. In instances of cleaning ambulance floors, counter tops, and seats that are not contaminated with blood, 1:100 bleach to water solution is appropriate. It is never appropriate to use a 100% bleach solution on anything. This may actually do more damage than good.

Questions

You arrive on the scene of a tanker truck carrying a hazardous material. You should position your vehicle

(A) 2,000 feet from the tanker truck.

(B) uphill.

(C) upwind.

(D) all of the above

Your Answer _____

_____

Career Pulse

EMTs may be paid or be volunteers in the community. Paramedics are paid providers.

Correct Answers

A–149

(D) If you are on the scene of a hazardous material incident, you should position your vehicle at least 2,000 feet from the incident. You should remain uphill to avoid any chance of a spill coming in contact with you. You should also be upwind so none of the vapors come through the air and in contact with you. You will need to monitor wind direction and may need to change locations if the wind changes.

Questions

You are treating a child that has bruises at various stages on their body. The child states that she keeps falling down. The patient has what appears to be a fractured wrist. You should

(A) confront the parents about your suspicion of child abuse.

(B) contact law enforcement and tell them of your suspicion.

(C) treat and transport the child; once at the hospital notify the physician, document your findings, and report the incident as required by your state.

(D) document the incident and allow your supervisor to make the decision of what to do after reading the patient care report.

Your Answer _____

_____

Correct Answers

A–150

(C)   Child abuse can be a very touchy situation. You do not want to confront the parents with your suspicion. The best way to handle this situation is to treat the patient and transport the patient to the appropriate facility. Do not let the child out of your sight. Once at the hospital, be sure to tell your findings to the physician, but do not be accusatory. Document your findings and make any notification to any state agency as required by your state.

Questions

Which of the following is NOT a primary function of an EMT-B?

(A) patient care

(B) document patient care

(C) billing the patient for services

(D) being a patient advocate

Your Answer _____

_____

Correct Answers

A–151

(C)   The functions of an EMT-B include: being prepared to treat patients, being ready to respond when called upon; respond, treat, and transport patients in a safe manner; properly assess your patients; provide prompt and effective patient care; lift and move patients safely; transfer patient care to one of the same level or greater level of care; document patient findings and history, and be a patient advocate. Many agencies bill for patient services; however, it is not a primary function of an EMT-B.

Questions

Which of the following does NOT fall within the scope of practice for an EMT-B?

(A) assessing a patient

(B) administering oxygen

(C) performing a cricothotomy

(D) using an AED

Your Answer _____

Correct Answers

A–152

(C) The scope of practice is what the EMT-B is permitted to do within the scope of their training and authorization of their medical director. It is an important concept to know and understand. EMT-Bs are not trained to perform a cricothotomys. By law, an EMT-B must perform their duties within their scope of practice.

Questions

When you grab a backboard, you realize that blood remains from an earlier call. With your hand covered in blood, your first step towards decontamination should be

(A) contacting your Infection Control Officer.

(B) washing your hands with soap and water.

(C) completing exposure control forms.

(D) going into the emergency department for admission.

Your Answer _____

_____

Correct Answers

A–153

(B) The first line of defense against any infectious disease that comes in contact with your intact skin is to wash it with soap and water. In most instances if you can immediately wash the intact skin surface with water and soap, there is a very good chance you will not be infected should the blood be contaminated with an infectious disease. Once you have thoroughly washed your hands or skin, you will then want to contact your Infection Control Officer and follow the appropriate protocols for the situation.

Questions

You arrive on the scene to find a 37-year-old male sitting on the couch. The patient states he has not felt well for a number of days. Complaining of fatigue, he is experiencing tenderness in the upper right quadrant of his abdomen. Upon further assessment, you notice that this patient's skin is jaundiced. You should suspect this patient to be

(A) HIV positive.

(B) suffering from TB.

(C) alcohol dependent.

(D) hepatitis positive.

Your Answer _____

Correct Answers

A–154

(D) This patient presents with classic signs of hepatitis, most likely hepatitis B positive. The key indicators are the fatigue, not feeling well, and tenderness in the upper right quadrant of the abdomen, which is where the liver is located. Hepatitis affects the liver. The jaundiced skin color is also indicative of hepatitis. The EMT-B needs to wear BSI and take universal precautions as he/she would with any other patients. A hepatitis B vaccine is also advisable, but needs to have been administered prior to this call.

Questions

$$\boxed{911}$$

Typically, which of the following is not one of the first things an EMT-B should do when arriving on the scene of an incident?

(A) assess the scene for hazards

(B) assess the patient's ABC's

(C) note the number of patients

(D) note the mechanism of injury

Your Answer _____

_____

Fast Fact

In 2001, males accounted for 78% of drownings in the United States. [http://www.cdc.gov/ncipc/factsheets/drown.htm]

Correct Answers

A–155

$$\boxed{911}$$

(B) When you arrive on the scene of any incident, you want to assess the scene for hazards and make sure the scene is safe before you approach the patient. Second, you want to note how many patients there are so you can determine the number of resources you need. Finally, you want to note the mechanism of injury, which will aid in the assessment of the patient. Assessing the patient's ABC's is important, but these three items need to be determined prior to even touching the patient.

Questions

911

There are five steps of grief associated with the death and dying process. The typical progression is

(A) denial, anger, bargaining, depression, and acceptance.

(B) anger, denial, bargaining, depression, and acceptance.

(C) denial, bargaining, anger, depression, and acceptance.

(D) depression, denial, anger, bargaining, and acceptance.

Your Answer _____

_____

Fast Fact

One of the first civilian EMS services can be traced back to 1869, when Dr. Edward L. Dalton at Bellevue Hospital in New York City, then known as the Free Hospital of New York, started a basic transportation service for the sick and injured. [http://en.wikipedia.org/wiki/Pre-hospital]

Correct Answers

911

(A) The stages of death and dying typically go through a process that begins with denial. It is the "not me" defense mechanism that builds a defense against reality. Next they experience anger—they do not deserve to die now. Then they begin to bargain, "I am ok with dying, but first let me...." Then they become depressed. They think of all the things they haven't done. And last, they accept the fact that they are going to die. These are typically the five stages and the progression that happens. On occasion, they may not get to the next stage or they may skip stages of the process. You may also find that it is not uncommon for the patient's loved ones to experience the five-stage process.

Questions

Which of the following signs and symptoms are associated with a response to a stressful situation?

(A) nausea/vomiting, shivering, diarrhea, dry mouth, and sweating

(B) nausea/vomiting, seizures, diarrhea, dry mouth, and sweating

(C) nausea/vomiting, shivering, diarrhea, excess saliva, and sweating

(D) nausea/vomiting, shivering, diarrhea, dry mouth, and seizures

Your Answer _____

_____

Correct Answers

(A) An EMT-B may experience a number of signs and symptoms when responding to an emergency or working at the scene of an incident that are normal responses to a stressful situation. They include: upset stomach, nausea and vomiting, shivering or shakes, feeling clumsy, diarrhea, dizziness, dry mouth, pounding heart, sweating, stomach cramping, and/or muscle aches.

Questions

An EMT-B can take steps towards managing and reducing the stress associated with working in the EMS environment. The following suggestions are all ways to assist in managing stress EXCEPT

(A) balancing your life with work, recreation, family and friends.

(B) drinking excessive amounts of alcohol to dull the pain of stress.

(C) keeping a positive attitude.

(D) realizing that your personality includes physical, mental, emotional, and spiritual needs.

Your Answer _____

_____

Career Pulse

EMS providers may be educated as First Responders (who have about 40 hours of training) along a continuum of training to Paramedics (who have about 1,000 or more hours of training).

Correct Answers

(B) It is important for the EMT-B to realize and recognize that managing stress is an important aspect of keeping your career in EMS a healthy one. A balance between work, recreation, family and friends is important to maintain this healthy lifestyle. By recognizing that your personality includes physical, mental, emotional, and spiritual needs, you can work towards rounding your activities to include these four areas. It is important to maintain a positive attitude. A positive attitude can also be infectious to those around you. You don't want to squelch your stress by alleviating it with alcohol.

Questions

There are two basic types of law, criminal law and civil law. A situation related to civil law is

(A) prison time for murdering another individual.

(B) an issued document that requires you to appear in court.

(C) a breach of contract.

(D) a traffic citation.

Your Answer _____

_____

Correct Answers

(C)   The easiest way to differentiate between civil and criminal law is that criminal is disciplinary in nature and civil law typically affects your pocketbook. In other words, if you are convicted of a criminal law you could be punished by imprisonment. It may also affect your pocketbook, if there is a fine associated with the punishment. Civil law, however does not carry any prison time associated with it. A breach of contract is an example of civil law, as are divorce and torts. An example to distinguish how one could be tried in both areas of law and found innocent of one and guilty of another is the infamous O.J. Simpson case. He was acquitted of any wrongdoing in the criminal trial and was found guilty in the civil proceedings.

Questions

Q–160

You arrive on the scene to discover a patient who refuses to allow you to touch her. You feel the patient is in need of treatment and attempt to take her blood pressure. You have just committed

(A) an assault.

(B) battery.

(C) negligence.

(D) an act befitting your profession.

Your Answer _____

Q–161

The skull is divided into four major areas. These four areas are called

(A) frontal, occipital, temporal, and lobal.

(B) frontal, occipital, temporal, and parietal.

(C) frontal, occipital, temporal, and partial.

(D) frontal, mandibular, temporal, and parietal.

Your Answer _____

Correct Answers

A–160

(B)   An assault is when you put the patient in immediate fear of harm versus battery which is touching the patient without their consent. Granted taking a blood pressure is within an EMT-B's scope of practice, however the patient refused to allow you to touch them. This is considered a battery and you could be criminally charged according to the law.

A–161

(B)   The skull is divided into four major areas. They are the frontal, which is the anterior section. The posterior section is called the occipital section. The sides are called the temporal section and the top section is called the parietal section.

Questions

The three main bones of the arm are the

(A) humerus, tibia, and radius.

(B) humerus, ulna, and fibula.

(C) humerus, tibia, and fibula.

(D) humerus, ulna, and radius.

Your Answer _____

_____

Career Pulse

About 4 out of 10 full-time and part-time paid EMTs and paramedics work as employees of private ambulance services.

Correct Answers

A–162

(D) The three main bones of the arm are the humerus, the ulna, and the radius. The femur, tibia, and the fibula are the three main bones of the leg.

Questions

You are assessing a patient's breathing. The four things you want to determine are

(A) rate, rhythm, quantity, and depth.

(B) rate, rhythm, quality, and depth.

(C) rate, rigidity, quantity, and depth.

(D) rate, rhythm, time, and depth.

Your Answer _____

_____

Correct Answers

A–163

(B) When assessing a patient's breathing you want to assess the respiratory rate or how many times the patient breathes in a one-minute period. You want to assess the patient's rhythm: is the patient breathing in normal breaths or breathing fast or slow? The quality of breathing is also important. Does the patient have a difficult time breathing? Last, assess the depth of the patient's breathing which is also known as the tidal volume. The patient may not be getting enough oxygen because they are not getting an adequate tidal volume.

Questions

You are providing rescue breathing to an adult patient using a mouth-to-barrier device. You should provide a tidal volume of

(A) 1600 to 2000 mL.

(B) 1300 to 1600 mL.

(C) 1000 to 1300 mL.

(D) 700 to 1000 mL.

Your Answer _____

_____

Fast Fact

EMTs and paramedics are often present at natural disasters such as floods, hurricanes, earthquakes, and ice storms; special events such as setting up stations at parades and marathons; and manmade disasters such as plane crashes, anthrax mailings, and terrorist events such as the Oklahoma City bombing and 9/11. [http://www.hhs.gov/news/press/ 2001pres/01fsemergencyresponse.html]

Correct Answers

A-164

(D) A common side effect from mouth-to-barrier ventilation is gastric distention so be careful how much volume of air you put into the patient. This can be prevented by giving approximately 700 to 1000 mL over a two-second period.

Questions

You are treating a patient with a laceration. You remember that _____ is/are the component within blood that is necessary to form a clot.

(A) red blood cells

(B) white blood cells

(C) platelets

(D) plasma

Your Answer _____

Correct Answers

(C)   Red blood cells make up the largest component of blood and are responsible for carrying oxygen and carbon dioxide to and from the tissues.
White blood cells exist to fight infections. Plasma
is a liquid in which blood cells and nutrients are
suspended. Therefore, platelets aid in the formation of clotting whenever they come in contact
with anything other than the lining of a blood vessel.

Questions

Which layer of the skin contains the sweat glands, sebaceous glands, hair follicles, blood vessels, and nerve endings?

(A) dermis

(B) epidermis

(C) subcutaneous

(D) subdermis

Your Answer _____

Career Pulse

About 3 out of 10 EMTs work in local government for fire departments, public ambulance services, and EMS.

Correct Answers

(A) The dermis contains the sweat glands, sebaceous glands, hair follicles, blood vessels, and nerve endings. The epidermis is the outermost layer of skin and consists of primarily dead cells, which provide a waterproof barrier. The subcutaneous layer is under the dermis and is made up of adipose, which is fat, and connective tissue.

Questions

You arrive on the scene to find an unconscious patient about 14 years of age. Where would you assess for a pulse on this patient?

(A) carotid artery

(B) brachial artery

(C) femoral artery

(D) radial artery

Your Answer _____

_____

Correct Answers

(A) This patient would be considered an adult and you would assess the carotid artery. A patient over the age of 8 is considered to be an adult in most cases in medicine. Patients from 1 to 8 are considered children and under 1 are considered to be infants. In infants and children, assess the pulse at the brachial artery. The femoral artery can be used to assess lower perfusion or to monitor effectiveness of CPR. Typically the femoral pulse is not used readily because of its location. The radial artery can be used to assess the rate of the heart, but should not be used to assess whether the patient has a heartbeat. There may not be a radial pulse but there may be a carotid pulse.

Questions

You are assessing a patient's blood pressure. The relaxation and refilling of the left ventricle is measured by the

(A) systolic pressure.

(B) diastolic pressure.

(C) pulse pressure.

(D) none of the above

Your Answer _____

_____

Fast Fact

Rural EMTs and paramedics face a different working environment than urban counterparts. They usually cover large areas with a low population density. [http://www.jems.com/jems/exclus04/e0104a. html]

Correct Answers

A–168

(B) The systolic pressure is the first sound heard when taking a blood pressure. It is the pressure created by the contraction of the left ventricle forcing blood into the body. The second sound, or actually when the sound stops, is the diastolic pressure. This occurs when the left ventricle relaxes and refills with blood. The pulse pressure is the difference between the systolic and the diastolic pressures.

Questions

When gathering a patient's medical history, the acronym SAMPLE is used. This acronym stands for

(A) signs and symptoms, allergies, medical history, previous occurrences, last oral intake, and events.

(B) stable or unstable, allergies, medications, pertinent medical history, last meal, and events.

(C) stable or unstable, allergies, medical history, pain description, last meal, and events.

(D) signs and symptoms, allergies, medications, pertinent medical history, last oral intake, and events.

Your Answer _____

Correct Answers

A-169

(D) SAMPLE stands for: Signs and symptoms—essentially your physical assessment of the patient. Allergies—is the patient allergic to anything? Medications—what medications does the patient take? Pertinent medical history—what medical history is pertinent to the care of the patient? Gall bladder surgery 20 years ago is typically not pertinent medical history; however if the surgery occurred six weeks ago, it may be very relevant. Last meal—when did the patient eat last? What did they have to eat? This may be what is ailing the patient whether they are having a reaction or they may be a diabetic who has failed to eat. Events is the last part of this assessment technique. Determining why EMS was called is an important aspect of your assessment. What events led up to the patient calling for EMS?

Questions

Q–170

Your patient is on the second floor of his home. While carrying, the patient should be moved

(A) feet first.

(B) head first.

(C) supine.

(D) none of the above

Your Answer _____

Q–171

911

Which of the following is not considered a significant mechanism of injury for an adult?

(A) roll-over of vehicle

(B) falls greater than 10 feet

(C) penetrations of head, chest, or abdomen

(D) ejection from vehicle

Your Answer _____

Correct Answers

A–170

(A) When moving a patient down the stairs, the patient should go feet first. When moving a patient up the stairs, the patient should go head first. This creates an environment that is most comfortable and least frightening for the patient. Most of your equipment is designed with this movement in mind.

A–171

(B) Falls greater than 10 feet are considered a significant mechanism of injury in a child or infant, but not in an adult. A fall greater than 20 feet is considered a significant mechanism of injury in an adult.

Questions

When you listen to the lungs of an asthma patient you would expect to hear

(A) wheezes.

(B) rales.

(C) stridor.

(D) rhonchi.

Your Answer _____

_____

Correct Answers

(A) Wheezes are indicative of asthma. In some instances they can be heard without the aid of a stethoscope. If the patient has a history of asthma but is not wheezing they could still be having an asthma attack. In severe cases the asthma progresses to a point where there is not wheezing. If the patient has a prescribed inhaler, contact medical control to get orders to assist in administering the inhaler.

Questions

$$\boxed{911}$$

Your patient is lying in the doorway of her home, which is on fire. You are first on scene. You should

(A) wait for the fire department.

(B) treat the patient where you found her.

(C) immediately move the patient.

(D) perform an initial assessment to determine what to do next.

Your Answer _____

_____

Career Pulse

About 2 out of 10 EMTs work full time either in hospitals or respond to calls in ambulances or helicopters to transport critically ill or injured patients.

Correct Answers

911

(C)   There are a few times when you will need to move the patient immediately; this is called an emergency move. As long as you can reach the patient and move them to safety, you should go ahead and perform the rescue. Since the patient is in the doorway and fire can be seen, an emergency move is appropriate in this scenario. If you arrive on the scene and the patient is still in the house, it is better to wait for fire personnel to arrive on the scene to perform the rescue. Never stay and treat a patient with impending danger, move to a safer spot.

Questions

You are treating an unresponsive patient and do not suspect that the patient has a neck or spinal injury. You should place this patient in which position?

(A) supine

(B) recovery

(C) prone

(D) trendelenburg

Your Answer _____

Correct Answers

(B) A patient who is unconscious and not suspected of having a spine or neck injury should be placed in the recovery position. When placing the patient in the recovery position, they should be placed on their left side so that when transported the patient will be facing the ambulance bench seat. The recovery position will aid in keeping the airway clear. The trendelenburg position is used for patients who are hypotensive. There are usually no incidents where you will want to transport a patient in the prone position. Exceptions would be an impaled object in the posterior part of the patient's body, and even then try to transport the patient on their side. Most patients are transported in the supine, fowlers, or semi-fowlers position.

Questions

You are treating a patient who becomes unresponsive. The patient was complaining of chest pain prior to becoming unresponsive. Your first step is to

(A) administer nitroglycerin.

(B) open the airway using the head-tilt chin lift.

(C) assess for a pulse.

(D) assess vital signs.

Your Answer _____

_____

Fast Fact

Almost 25% of all patients transported by EMS are suffering from some form of moderate to severe pain. [http://www2.us.elsevierhealth.com]

Correct Answers

(B) When treating a patient who becomes unconscious, your first priority is to ensure an open airway. Unless you suspect the patient has a possible
c-spine injury, you would open the airway with the
head-tilt chin-lift method. After you get their airway open, then assess for breathing. Never give an
unconscious patient anything by mouth.

Questions

You are suctioning your patient's airway. One of the biggest side effects of suctioning is

(A) hypoxia.

(B) aspiration.

(C) suctioning power.

(D) suction catheter clogging.

Your Answer _____

_____

Fast Fact

Two levels of care are provided by EMS systems: BLS (Basic Life Support) and ALS (Advanced Life Support). [http://en.wikipedia.org/wiki/Pre-hospital]

Correct Answers

A–176

(A) The greatest concern when suctioning is hypoxia. Suction for no more than 15 seconds at a time and then attempt ventilations. There are incidents when continuous suctioning may be needed, however, keep in mind, the patient's state of hypoxia becomes increasingly worse. The suction catheter clogging is another concern, but it is not the greatest concern. It is much easier to replace the suction catheter than caring for a patient who becomes more hypoxic. Likewise, suction power is not a major concern, but enough suction is needed to remove the foreign material. Typically 300 mm Hg is required for suction units to function properly. Aspiration is also a problem, however, by suctioning, you are hopefully reducing or eliminating this problem and not causing it to occur.

Questions

A common method for documenting a patient assessment on a patient care report form is

(A) DCAPP BTLS.

(B) SOAP.

(C) ABCDE.

(D) OPQRST.

Your Answer _____

Correct Answers

(B) The SOAP method is a common method to document your patient care. It covers the majority of your findings and treatment. **S** is for subjective or the information the patient tells you. **O** is for objective or your findings upon assessing the patient. **A** is for Assessment or your evaluation of the patient. The **P** is for your plan or the action you are going to take as the EMT-B to care for this patient. DCAPP BTLS is an acronym used during your physical assessment to remember what you are assessing for—Deformities, Abrasions, Punctures, Penetrations, Burns, Tenderness, Lacerations, and Swelling. ABC is for your assessment of the Airway, Breathing, and Circulation. OPQRST could be another means for documentation, however this typically refers to assessment of pain. It stands for **O**nset, **P**rovocation, **Q**uality, **R**adiate, **S**everity, and **T**ime. You may use this as a guide in your documentation, but is not the best format for documentation in this question.

Questions

Your patient has been having seizures without gaining responsiveness between the seizures. You are concerned about protecting his airway. You want to insert a nasopharyngeal airway. To properly size the airway you should

(A) measure from the tip of the ear to the tip of the nose.

(B) measure from the tip of the ear to the tip of the mouth.

(C) measure from the tip of the nose to the tip of the chin.

(D) measure from the tip of the nose to the corner of the mouth to the tip of the ear.

Your Answer _____

_____

Correct Answers

A–178

(A) In order to insert the proper nasopharyngeal airway, measure from the tip of the ear to the tip of the nose. If inserting an oropharyngeal airway, measure from the corner of the mouth to the tip of the ear.

Questions

You are using a flow-restricted oxygen-powered ventilator. To prevent gastric distention, the maximum flow rate should be set at

(A) 10 L/min.
(B) 15 L/min.
(C) 30 L/min.
(D) 40 L/min.

Your Answer _____

_____

Career Pulse

Earnings of EMTs and paramedics depend on the employment setting and geographic location as well as the individual's training and experience.

Correct Answers

A–179

(D) Gastric distention is a concern when using a flow-restricted oxygen-powered ventilator. The flow rate should not be set any greater than 40 L/min.

Questions

To decrease gastric distention during artificial ventilation, you should

(A) apply the Sellick maneuver.

(B) decrease the amount of ventilation you administer.

(C) tilt the patient's head back further.

(D) apply pressure to the abdomen.

Your Answer _____

Correct Answers

A–180

(A) In order to decrease gastric distention and the possibility of the patient regurgitating and aspirating their vomit, you should use the Sellick maneuver. This is accomplished by applying pressure to the cricoid cartilage just below the Adam's Apple. You should not push on the patient's stomach if they do have gastric distention. Remember, what goes in must come out and there will be vomitus that comes back out with the air from the stomach. Be sure to have your suction unit close by.

Questions

911

You arrive on the scene to find a patient with lacerations to her arms and legs. During your initial assessment the patient's husband begins wielding a knife at you and tells you to leave her alone or he will stab you. You should

(A) continue treating the patient.

(B) retreat to a safe location and wait for law enforcement.

(C) have your partner approach the husband and try to reason with him.

(D) attempt to get the knife from the patient.

Your Answer _____

_____

Correct Answers

A–181

$$\boxed{911}$$

(B) Any time the scene is not safe leave the scene immediately. Granted there will be incidents where the EMT-B will be in risky situations. Every call could potentially go bad. This particular incident has gone bad and the EMT-B needs to retreat to a safe location and notify law enforcement. Once law enforcement secures the scene, the patient. Never attempt to disarm anyone. Law enforcement officers are specially trained to do this.

Questions

You are treating a patient at a local restaurant. An individual approaches you and tells you he is a doctor. You should

(A) allow the physician to take over since he is more qualified.

(B) have the physician perform invasive skills that you cannot perform.

(C) ask the physician for his credentials and follow your protocols.

(D) allow the physician to help you on the scene and then transport the patient to the hospital without the physician.

Your Answer _____

_____

Correct Answers

A–182

(C)   The first thing you want to find out is if the doctor is indeed a doctor and what type of doctor. A podiatrist will not be very helpful for a patient who is having chest pain, nor will a cardiologist be helpful for a patient having a baby. It is imperative that all local protocols are followed and that the physician accompany the patient to the hospital to assume all medical and legal responsibilities for the patient.

Questions

Your patient is unresponsive and responds whenever you pinch his feet. This patient's level of consciousness is classified as

(A) **A** - **A**lert.

(B) **V** - Responds to **V**erbal Stimulus.

(C) **P** - Responds to **P**ainful Stimulus.

(D) **U** - **U**nresponsive.

Your Answer _____

Correct Answers

(**C**) AVPU is used to assess the patient's level of consciousness. A is for alert—the patient is awake and talking to you though they may not respond appropriately. V is for verbal stimulus—when a patient only responds upon your verbal command. P is for painful stimulation, which is the case in this scenario, when the patient responds to you after you inflict pain. Again, the patient may not communicate verbally to you, but they do pull back or withdraw when you inflict the painful stimulus. U is for unresponsive. These are patients that do not respond to you by any of the means mentioned above.

Questions

You are treating a patient with shortness of breath. You want to deliver 15 L/min of oxygen at 100%. You should deliver this flow rate with a

(A) nasal cannula.

(B) simple face mask.

(C) partial re-breather mask.

(D) non-rebreather mask.

Your Answer _____

_____

Fast Fact

Once thought of as an ambulance driver or attendant, the modern EMT performs many duties, and responds to many types of emergency calls, including medical emergencies, hazardous materials exposure, childbirth, child abuse, fires, injuries, trauma and psychiatric crises. [http://en.wikipedia.org]

Correct Answers

(D)   In order to deliver 100% of oxygen at 15 L/min use a non-rebreather mask. Any of the other masks will not deliver 100% oxygen but are capable of flowing 15 L/min. A nasal cannula should have a maximum flow rate of 6 L/min.

Questions

Q-185

During your assessment of a patient's chest you note that the left side of the chest moves opposite to the right. This is called

(A) crepitus.

(B) paradigmal motion.

(C) subcutaneous emphysema.

(D) paradoxical movement.

Your Answer _____

_____

Q-186

During an assessment you note a pulsating mass in the mid-upper portion of the abdomen. This is most likely indicative of a(n)

(A) bruit.

(B) ruptured liver.

(C) abdominal pulse.

(D) aneurysm.

Your Answer _____

_____

Correct Answers

A–185

(D)   When the patient's left or right chest moves the opposite of the other side, this is referred to paradoxical movement. In most instances this is indicative of a flailed segment. Crepitus and subcutaneous emphysema may be additional signs of the flailed segment.

A–186

(D)   A pulsating mass in the area is typically indicative of an aneurysm. An aneurysm is a blood vessel that has a weakened area that has ballooned out. It is similar to a bicycle tire that becomes weak in one area and a bulge occurs. The bulge lasts only for a short time before it ruptures. This is the same with an aneurysm.

Questions

When delivering your report to the receiving hospital over the radio, you should report all the following EXCEPT

(A) your unit number.

(B) the patient's sex and age.

(C) the patient's name.

(D) the patient's current illness.

Your Answer _____

Career Pulse

Median annual earnings of EMTs and paramedics were $24,030 in 2002. The middle 50 percent earned between $19,040 and $31,600. The lowest 10 percent earned less than $15,530, and the highest 10 percent earned more than $41,980.

Correct Answers

A–187

(C)   When giving a report to the receiving hospital by radio you should give the following information: Your unit number, your level of certification, ETA, age and sex of the patient, chief complaint, brief pertinent history of the present illness, major past illnesses, mental status, baseline vital signs, pertinent findings, medical care given, and response to the medical treatment. You should never give the patient's name over the radio. This may be seen as a breach of patient confidentiality.

Questions

While treating a patient with shortness of breath, you administer oxygen based on written guidelines from your medical director. You administer the oxygen based on

(A) protocols or standing orders.

(B) on-line medical direction.

(C) your EMT-B textbook.

(D) the Medical Practice Care Act.

Your Answer _____

Correct Answers

A–188

(A) Your care is typically based upon written protocols or standing orders by your medical director. These are also referred to as off-line medical direction. On-line medical direction is when you contact the medical director for direction on how to care for the patient via a radio or telephone.

Questions

You arrive on the scene of an auto accident. There is one vehicle and an 18-year-old patient. The police officer advises you that the patient is fine and that she does not want any treatment, on scene or at a hospital. You should

(A) explain the consequences of not being treated and brought to a hospital and have the patient sign a refusal.

(B) have the police officer sign the refusal form stating the patient does not want to go to the hospital.

(C) begin assessing and treating the patient regardless, since the patient looks as though she may have been injured.

(D) refrain from making any physical contact with the patient and notify dispatch that you have been cancelled by law enforcement.

Your Answer _____

_____

Correct Answers

A–189

(A) In many instances law enforcement personnel are not medically trained and you should not
rely on them to provide medical care. In this scenario, the most appropriate step is to explain to the
patient directly the consequences of refusing patient care and transport and have her sign a refusal
form. It is also advisable that you have at least one
witness sign to attest to this. There are many EMT-
B's who would elect to do the last answer. That is
not proper patient care and many of these EMT-B's
have found themselves in a court of law for taking
this action. When you are called to the scene of an
incident, you have a duty to act and if you do not
act, you may be charged for those inactions.

Questions

You arrive on the scene to find a patient with troubled breathing and chest pain. Upon assessment of the patient, she tells you that she had a salad for lunch at a local seafood restaurant. She notes during the assessment that she is allergic to shellfish. Upon further assessment you note hives around their mouth. You should consider treating this patient by

(A) assisting her in taking one of her nitroglycerin tablets.

(B) assisting her in taking her prescribed inhaler.

(C) assisting her in taking her antacid.

(D) assisting her in administering a prescribed epinephrine injector.

Your Answer _____

_____

Correct Answers

(D) This patient appears to be having an allergic reaction. The shortness of breath and chest pain are symptoms of the allergic reaction. The key is that the patient ate at a seafood restaurant and is allergic to shellfish. Upon assessment you also noted the hives which is indicative of an allergic reaction. Many restaurants have shellfish added in the salad without most individuals knowing. The most appropriate care for this patient is to assist in administering their epinephrine injector. Remember that it has to be prescribed to them and you need to get the approval from your medical director before administering the medication.

Questions

You are treating a patient who ingested a poison. Poison Control advises you that this poison is best treated with Activated Charcoal. Activated Charcoal works by

(A) adsorption.

(B) inducing vomiting.

(C) absorption.

(D) inducing urination.

Your Answer _____

You are treating a diabetic and consider administering glucose to the patient. Glucose will

(A) lower the blood sugar.

(B) raise the blood sugar.

(C) lower the insulin levels.

(D) raise the insulin levels.

Your Answer _____

Correct Answers

A–191

(A) Activated Charcoal works by adsorbing the substance. Syrup of Ipecac works by inducing vomiting. There are really no side effects to Activated Charcoal which is a slurry mixture that can be very messy and does not taste good.

A–192

(B) Glucose is used to raise the blood sugar. Regardless of whether the patient is hypoglycemic or hyperglycemic, it will not hurt the patient to give them oral glucose. A patient that is hypoglycemic is in dire need of glucose and it is critical that they get the glucose in a short amount of time. A patient who is hyperglycemic will not be affected in a dire way by getting more glucose. At no time should an EMT-B give or assist in giving insulin. This is a very potent drug and can cause severe side effects if given improperly.

Questions

Albuterol is a medication administered by
(A) injection.
(B) inhalation.
(C) absorption.
(D) orally.

Your Answer _____

You are treating an elderly patient who has a fever, chills, cough with sputum production, and dyspnea. The patient also states that the symptoms have been progressing rapidly and you note breathing is difficult. This patient is most likely suffering from
(A) pneumonia.
(B) COPD.
(C) emphysema.
(D) tuberculosis.

Your Answer _____

Correct Answers

A–193

(B) Albuterol is given by inhalation. It is a medication for the treatment of breathing disorders, usually associated with asthma. It helps open the airways in the lungs, thus allowing for easier breathing.

A–194

(A) These are characteristic signs of pneumonia. The key here is the fever and chills. Pneumonia is typically caused by an infection which is indicated by fever. The treatment for this patient is general supportive care, including oxygen and transport to the hospital. This patient should be transported in at least a semi-Fowlers position to aid breathing.

Questions

You are treating a 5-year-old patient who has a foreign body partially obstructing his airway. You would suspect to hear

(A) wheezes.

(B) rales.

(C) stridor.

(D) rhonchi.

Your Answer _____

The following are causes of pulmonary edema EXCEPT

(A) congestive heart failure.

(B) severe infection.

(C) smoke inhalation.

(D) an embolism.

Your Answer _____

Correct Answers

A–195

(C) Stridor is a high-pitched harsh sound heard during inspiration, which results from a narrowing in the upper airway. This is usually a result of a foreign body partially obstructing the airway. It is also commonly heard as a result of an infection, such as croup or epiglottitis.

A–196

(D) There are many conditions that cause pulmonary edema. The most common cause is congestive heart failure. Other conditions include: severe infections, smoke or toxic inhalations, high altitudes, narcotic overdoses, and fluid overload.

Questions

You are called to a local high school where you find a 17-year-old female breathing at a rate of 40 breaths per minute. She is complaining of tingling in her hands and feet and appears very agitated. You were told by her friend that she just broke up with her boyfriend. You suspect this patient is suffering from

(A) hyperventilation.

(B) severe episode of dyspnea.

(C) an asthma attack.

(D) drug overdose.

Your Answer _____

_____

Correct Answers

A–197

(A) This patient appears to be suffering from a classic case of hyperventilation. Patients who are breathing very fast, have tingling or numbness in their feet and hands, along with being agitated, and having a hunger for air are usually suffering from hyperventilation. This is usually a result of an emotional upset, as in this case.

Questions

Q–198

The treatment for the patient in the previous question would be to

(A) have the patient breath in a paper bag.

(B) reassure and calm the patient.

(C) administer oxygen 6 L/min.

(D) administer oxygen 15 L/min.

Your Answer _____

_____

Q–199

You arrive on the scene of a 2 year old that has a barking cough, low-grade fever, and cold-like symptoms. You suspect this child is suffering from

(A) asthma.

(B) bronchitis.

(C) epiglottitis.

(D) croup.

Your Answer _____

_____

Correct Answers

A–198

(B) It is no longer appropriate to have a patient breath into a paper bag. In this particular case, the most appropriate means of treatment is to calm and reassure the patient. Hyperventilation can also occur in diabetic patients who are in a diabetic coma. In this particular situation or when you are unsure why the patient is hyperventilating, you should not withhold oxygen.

A–199

(D) These are classic signs and symptoms of a patient with croup. The age of the patient is usually from 6 months to 3 years.

Questions

Which of the following arrhythmias should be shocked using an AED?

(A) asystole

(B) ventricular tachycardia

(C) pulseless electrical activity

(D) atrial fibrillation

Your Answer _____

_____

Fast Fact

Oxygen administration is a first aid treatment for emergencies involving the organs of respiration and circulation such as heart attack, drowning, carbon monoxide poisoning, decompression illness, lung barotraumas, and gas embolism. [http://en.wikipedia.org]

Correct Answers

A–200

(B) Ventricular tachycardia without a pulse should be shocked using an AED. Any rhythm that has a disorganized electrical activity coupled with no pulse should be shocked using an AED. The other rhythm that is shocked on a common basis is ventricular fibrillation. Pulseless Electrical Activity, or PEA, has an organized electrical activity. In this rhythm, the patient has an underlying problem that needs to be resolved and defibrillation is not appropriate. A patient in asystole does not have any electrical activity and a shock will not benefit this patient. Atrial fibrillation is not a rhythm that an EMT-B will shock.

Questions

You are treating a 45-year-old male who has a history of heart problems. The patient tells you that he has chest pain after exerting himself, however it relieves itself when he rests. You would suspect this patient has

(A) angina pectoris.

(B) myocardial infarction.

(C) congestive heart failure.

(D) muscular skeletal pain.

Your Answer _____

_____

Career Pulse

Advancement beyond the EMT-Paramedic level usually means leaving fieldwork. An EMT-Paramedic can become a supervisor, operations manager, administrative director, or executive director of emergency services.

Correct Answers

A–201

(A) This patient has the signs and symptoms of angina pectoris. Chest pain brought on by exercise or exertion and relieved by resting is indicative of angina. This is caused by the narrowing of the blood vessels which is typically a result of atherosclerosis.

Questions

The patient in the previous question may also have his chest pain relieved by

(A) Albuterol.

(B) lasix.

(C) epinephrine.

(D) nitroglycerin.

Your Answer _____

_____

Correct Answers

A–202

(D) Patients suffering from angina and who have had this condition in the past will typically have nitroglycerin prescribed to them. If the patient is still having chest pain, contact your medical director to get orders to assist the patient in taking his prescribed nitroglycerin. It is important that patients take medication that is prescribed only to them.

Questions

Which of the following patients should you connect to an AED?

(A) 50-year-old unresponsive male.

(B) 4-year-old unresponsive female with a pulse.

(C) 45-year-old male complaining of chest pain.

(D) 52-year-old female complaining of a fast heart beat.

Your Answer _____

_____

Fast Fact

Administration of oxygen is also helpful in multiple trauma patients, unresponsive patients of unknown history, and diabetic emergencies. [http://en.wikipedia.org]

Correct Answers

A–203

(A) The most appropriate patient is the 50-year-old male who is unresponsive. There is never a reason to connect an AED to a conscious patient regardless of their chief complaint. This is a question you cannot read anything into but take at face value and select the most appropriate answer.

Questions

You are treating a patient who appears to be having symptoms of a myocardial infarction. You know that one of the serious problems that a myocardial infarction may lead to is

(A) angina pectoris.

(B) ventricular fibrillation.

(C) ischemia.

(D) cardiac tamponade.

Your Answer _____

Correct Answers

A–204

(B) One of the most serious problems or conditions that a myocardial infarction can lead to is cardiac arrest with ventricular fibrillation being the most common arrhythmia associated. If the patient goes unresponsive, it is essential you apply your AED immediately. Immediate defibrillation can be a life saver for these patients. Early defibrillation saves lives.

Questions

Q–205

You are treating a 62-year-old female patient who is complaining of shortness of breath, chest pain and is coughing up a pink frothy sputum. You would suspect this patient has

(A) right sided congestive heart failure.

(B) left sided congestive heart failure.

(C) emphysema.

(D) pneumonia.

Your Answer _____

_____

Career Pulse

Some EMTs and paramedics become instructors, dispatchers, or physician assistants, while others move into sales or marketing of emergency medical equipment.

Correct Answers

A–205

(B) This patient is suffering from congestive heart failure. In order to know if it is right or left depends on the patient's symptoms. In this case the patient has pink frothy sputum which is indicative of oxygenated blood. Essentially the left side of the heart is not able to keep and the blood backs up into the lungs and causes the pink frothy sputum. Right sided heart failure is when the right side of the heart cannot keep up with the blood flow and you typically see JVD.

Questions

The treatment for the previous patient would be to

(A) administer oxygen at 6 L/min and transport in the supine position.

(B) administer oxygen at 6 L/min and transport in the Fowlers position.

(C) administer oxygen at 15 L/min and transport in the Fowlers position.

(D) administer oxygen at 15 L/min and transport in the supine position.

Your Answer _____

_____

Correct Answers

(C) This patient needs 100% supplemental oxygen delivered at 15 L/min via non-rebreather mask. The patient should also be transported in the Fowlers or sitting position. If you put the patient in a supine position, they will feel like they are drowning. By placing them in the Fowler's position it allows the fluid in the lungs to migrate to the lower portion of the lung and assist in their breathing.

Questions

Q–207

A patient who is in a state of hypoperfusion caused by inadequate pumping action by the heart is known as

(A) cardiac introphy.

(B) cardiogenic arrest.

(C) cardiogenic shock.

(D) cardiac tamponade.

Your Answer _____

_____

Fast Fact

As of 2003, the busiest EMS service per ambulance is New Orleans' Health Department EMS, which responds to approximately 4,000 "911" calls per month, utilizing six ambulances for the entire city of about 500,000 people. [http://en.wikipedia.org]

Correct Answers

A–207

(C) This is the definition of cardiogenic shock. The pump has been damaged and cannot keep up with the blood flow causing the patient to go into shock, hence cardiogenic shock.

Questions

You are treating a patient with chest pain and know there are some contraindications to the administration of nitroglycerin. Which of the following is not a contraindication to the administration of nitroglycerin?

(A) The patient is twenty years old.

(B) The patient's systolic pressure is 90.

(C) The patient has taken three nitroglycerin tablets.

(D) The patient has a head injury.

Your Answer _____

_____

Correct Answers

(A) Contraindications of nitroglycerin are: systolic blood pressure less than 100 mm Hg, a head injury, an infant or child patient, and/or the patient has taken three nitroglycerin tablets prior to your arrival. A twenty-year-old typically does not have a heart attack, however it is possible, and there is no contraindication for their age.

Questions

After administering a nitroglycerin tablet to the 50-year-old female patient you are caring for, your next step would be to

(A) give the patient another nitroglycerin if they continue to have chest pain.

(B) ask the patient to chew the tablet so it is absorbed.

(C) wait two minutes and take the patient's blood pressure.

(D) check the date the nitroglycerin was filled.

Your Answer _____

_____

Correct Answers

A–209

(C) After giving a patient their nitroglycerin you should take their blood pressure approximately two minutes after administration. It is important to monitor a patient's blood pressure because nitroglycerin can cause patients to become hypotensive. You should check the dates on the medication bottle prior to giving the medication. It is important to check the dates but it is too late after you have given the medication. Nitroglycerin is administered sublingually, which means placing the tablet under the tongue and allowing it to dissolve. Never have the patient chew the tablet and do not give another nitroglycerin immediately. Check the patient's blood pressure and monitor changes in the patient. Nitroglycerin can be administered every 3 to 5 minutes until the pain is relieved, the patient has taken three nitroglycerin tablets or the systolic blood pressure is less than 100 mm Hg.

Questions

Q–210

In treating a patient in cardiac arrest, you applied the AED and have delivered one shock. The patient now has a pulse. Next, you should stop CPR and
(A) monitor the patient.
(B) reassess the patient's breathing.
(C) transport immediately.
(D) continue assisting ventilations.

Your Answer _____

Q–211

You and your partner are administering chest compressions to a 57-year-old male. The rate of compressions would be
(A) no more than 80 compressions per minute.
(B) no less than 120 compressions per minute.
(C) at least 70 compressions per minute.
(D) no more than 100 compressions per minute.

Your Answer _____

Correct Answers

A-210

(B) The next step is to reassess your patient. Even though the patient has a pulse, they may or may not have started breathing on their own. Any time the patient's condition changes, you should reassess the patient and treat accordingly. In this case reassess the breathing and continue care according to your findings.

A-211

(D) The rate of compressions for an adult patient is 80 to 100 compressions per minute.

Questions

The ratio of chest compressions to ventilations for a
child during two-rescuer CPR as a health provider is
(A)15:2.
(B) 3:1.
(C) 4:1.
(D) 5:1.

Your Answer _____

The rate for rescue breathing in an infant is
(A) 1:1-3.
(B) 1:2-4.
(C) 1:3-5.
(D) 1:4-6.

Your Answer _____

Correct Answers

A–212

(A) The ratio of compressions to ventilations is 1 to 2. In other words, compress the chest 15 times; then the second rescuer gives two breaths.

A–213

(C) The rate for rescue breathing in an infant is one breath every three to five seconds, or 12 to 20 breaths per minute. 1:3-5.

Questions

Q–214

You are doing two-rescuer CPR as a health care provider. You should switch between compressions and ventilations every
(A) one minute.
(B) two minutes.
(C) five minutes.
(D) when one of you gets tired.

Your Answer _____

Q–215

The production of insulin occurs in the
(A) pancreas.
(B) liver.
(C) gall bladder.
(D) kidney.

Your Answer _____

Correct Answers

A–214

(B) You should switch between performing compressions and administering ventilations every two minutes. It has been found that the most effective compressions can only be given by one person for a two-minute period.

A–215

(A) The production of insulin occurs in the pancreas.

Questions

You are called to the scene of a female patient in her twenties who has an altered level of consciousness. Her boyfriend tells you that she takes insulin and has taken it as prescribed. He notes that they have been gone most of the day and she missed eating lunch. He said her glucose meter registered low when he took it. You would suspect this patient is

(A) overdosed on her insulin.

(B) intoxicated.

(C) hyperglycemic.

(D) hypoglycemic.

Your Answer _____

Correct Answers

A–216

(D) Patients with low blood sugar are considered hypoglycemic. These episodes usually come on quickly as a result of the patient taking insulin but not eating. Patients who are hyperglycemic or have high blood sugar tend to have their symptoms occur over time. Hypoglycemic patients need immediate treatment as this can be fatal if not treated in a timely fashion.

Questions

You are treating a diabetic patient and his wife tells you that the doctor said the patient is not insulin dependent. You know this kind of diabetes is
(A) Type II.
(B) Type I.
(C) Type IV.
(D) Type III.

Your Answer _____

_____

Career Pulse

EMTs and paramedics should be emotionally stable, have good dexterity, agility, and physical coordination, and be able to lift and carry heavy loads. They also need good eyesight (corrective lenses may be used) with accurate color vision.

Correct Answers

A–217

(A) Type II is known as non-insulin dependent diabetes. It usually occurs later in life and is associated with obesity. Type I is known as insulin dependent diabetes and typically occurs in adolescence or early adulthood. Type I is thought to occur as a result of a virus that damages the pancreas.

Questions

You are treating a patient suffering from anaphylactic shock. Which of the signs and symptoms would you likely see in this patient?

(A) urticaria, bradycardia, tachypnea, and stridor

(B) subcutaneous emphysema, bradycardia, dyspnea, and wheezing

(C) urticaria, hypertension, tachypnea, and tachycardia

(D) urticaria, tachycardia, tachypnea, and hypotension

Your Answer _____

Correct Answers

(D) Patients who are suffering from anaphylactic shock may exhibit a variety of signs and symptoms depending on the severity and the stage it is in. Patients typically have urticaria or hives, will be tachycardic, and may have tachypnea. In the late stages the patient will be hypotensive and have stridor as a result of the upper airway swelling closed.

Questions

Which of the following is NOT a contraindication of administering Syrup of Ipecac?
(A) ingestion of caustic materials
(B) ingestion of hydrocarbons
(C) ingestion of antihypertensive medications
(D) tricyclic antidepressant medications

Your Answer _____

_____

Correct Answers

(C) Syrup of Ipecac is a controversial medication and is not widely used any longer. You may still be called upon to administer it and need to know the contraindications of using it. It should not be used with patients that have ingested caustic material or hydrocarbons. Any ingested material or medication that could rapidly lead to a change in mental status, such as a tricyclic antidepressants that can cause seizures without warning, is a contraindication in administering Syrup of Ipecac. Also, patients who have ingested any material a significant time prior to emergency care should not be administered Syrup of Ipecac.

Questions

You are treating a patient with frostbite. Which of the following actions should be taken?
(A) Break any blisters on the wound.
(B) Apply direct heat to the affected area.
(C) Rub or massage the affected area.
(D) Remove any jewelry from the afflicted limb.

Your Answer _____

_____

Fast Fact

CPR stands for **C**ardio**P**ulmonary
Resuscitation. It is emergency first aid for an
unconscious person on whom breathing and a pulse
cannot be detected. The medical term for this condition
is cardiac arrest or, if the patient still has a pulse,
respiratory arrest (the combined term cardiorespiratory
arrest is also used). [http://en.wikipedia.org/wiki/
Cardiopulmonary_resuscitation]

Correct Answers

A–220

(D) When treating a patient with frostbite you should AVOID breaking any of the blisters, directly applying heat or rewarming the body part, and rubbing or massaging the affected areas. Also, unless following prescribed guidelines, do not allow the patient to walk on or use the affected extremity. You should remove jewelry since swelling commonly occurs with frostbite and may further impede circulation to the limb. The frostbite should be covered with dry sterile dressings.

Questions

You are a called to the scene of a possible poisoning. Upon arrival the patient is lying at the doorway of a lab. The patient is unconscious and you notice chemicals spilled in the room. Your next step would be to

(A) open the patient's airway.

(B) remove the patient to another area.

(C) identify the chemical.

(D) do a rapid assessment.

Your Answer _____

Correct Answers

A–221

(B) If you can safely remove a patient from a hazardous environment, do that first. If you cannot, retreat to a safe environment and call for additional help. It does not matter if the patient is breathing, has a pulse, or whatever if they are in a hazardous environment. Remember scene safety.

Questions

Which of the following is the correct dose of activated charcoal for an adult patient?
(A) 12.5 to 25 g.
(B) 25 to 50 g.
(C) 50 to 75 g.
(D) 75 to 100 g.

Your Answer _____

Which of the following heat emergencies is considered a true emergency?
(A) heat cramps
(B) heat exhaustion
(C) heat infarction
(D) heat stroke

Your Answer _____

Correct Answers

A–222

(B) The correct dosage of activated charcoal for an adult is 25 to 50 g. For a pediatric patient it is 12.5 to 25 g.

A–223

(D) Heat strokes are considered a true life threatening emergency. A heat stroke typically occurs after the patient has experienced heat cramps and heat exhaustion. A heat stroke patient has hot, dry skin. They no longer are sweating. This will progress to seizures and unresponsiveness. Death is imminent without appropriate and immediate treatment.

Questions

911

You are treating a patient who has overdosed on a narcotic. The greatest risk for this patient is
(A) respiratory depression.
(B) seizures.
(C) hypertension.
(D) hyperactivity.

Your Answer _____

911

A 7-year-old burns her hand on a stove burner. This is an example of what type of heat transfer?
(A) convection
(B) radiation
(C) conduction
(D) evaporation

Your Answer _____

Correct Answers

A–224

911

(A) The most important thing to note with a narcotic overdose is respiratory depression, which may lead to airway compromise. Narcotic medications depress the mental status of the patient.

A–225

911

(C) This is an example of conduction which is the direct heat exchange that occurs when two or more different temperature surfaces come into direct contact. The temperature tries to equate by transferring the heat to the cooler object or the cooler object attempts to reduce the hotter object.

Questions

Which of the following would provide you with the greatest information when dealing with a poison patient?

(A) medical director
(B) chemtrec
(C) hazcon
(D) poison control center

Your Answer _____

_____

Correct Answers

A–226

(D) Your greatest resource for information regarding a patient who has a poisoning emergency is the poison control center. Your medical director is a wealth of information but he too relies on the poison control center for information when dealing with poison patients.

Questions

A 27-year-old patient states that he opened the oven door and was burned from the heat of the oven. This is an example of what type of heat transfer?

(A) convection
(B) radiation
(C) conduction
(D) evaporation

Your Answer _____

_____

Fast Fact

Correct Answers

(B) Radiation is when heat is transferred or lost in the form of heat waves through air or water. The heat moves from the patient to other objects without direct contact. Convection creates heat loss by air currents moving across an exposed surface area. Evaporation is the changing of a liquid into a gas, which requires heat. A common example of this type of heat loss is when the body tries to cool itself by sweating.

Questions

Your patient is suffering from frostbite. You would expect to see the following signs and symptoms:

(A) blue-grayish skin; blisters filled with fluid; pitted edema

(B) ice covered skin; erupted blisters; skin hard to the touch

(C) white, waxy skin; fluid-filled blisters; skin hard to the touch

(D) blue skin; erupted blisters; pitted edema

Your Answer _____

Career Pulse

Competition is greater for EMT jobs in local government, including fire, police, and independent third-service rescue squad departments, in which salaries and benefits tend to be slightly better.

Correct Answers

(C) Deep frostbite has signs and symptoms that include: white and waxy skin, the skin is hard to the touch, gross swelling, and fluid-filled blisters. If the skin becomes thawed or partially thawed, the skin may appear cyanotic or flushed with mottled areas.

Questions

911

A patient has suffered a burn that involves the epidermis, dermis, and the hypodermis. This is classified as a

(A) full thickness burn.
(B) partial thickness burn.
(C) superficial burn.
(D) dermis burn.

Your Answer _____

_____

Fast Fact

Pittsburgh, Penn., Portland, Ore., and Seattle, Wash., were early pioneers in prehospital emergency medical training. [http://en.wikipedia.org/wiki/Paramedic]

Correct Answers

$$\boxed{911}$$

(A) A full thickness burn involves all the layers of the skin and the portion under the skin referred to as the hypodermis. This involves the nerves, therefore the patient will not complain of pain around the full thickness burn area.

Questions

911

You are assisting a patient who had a flash burn to both of his hands. The patient has charring of the skin and tissue damage through the skin and the underlying tissues. These signs and symptoms are indicative of a

(A) full thickness burn.
(B) partial thickness burn.
(C) superficial burn.
(D) dermis burn.

Your Answer _____

_____

Career Pulse

Career opportunities are best for those who have advanced certifications, such as EMT-Intermediate and EMT-Paramedic, as clients and patients demand higher levels of care before arriving at the hospital.

Correct Answers

A–230

$$\boxed{911}$$

(A) This patient has the signs and symptoms indicative of a full thickness burn.

Questions

911

You respond to a structure fire. When you arrive on the scene a firefighter brings you a 57-year-old male. He has partial and full thickness burns to his arms and legs. You note partial thickness burns around his mouth and forehead. Your first priority with this patient is to

(A) apply burn dressings.
(B) open the patient's airway.
(C) maintain body temperature.
(D) transport the patient to the burn hospital.

Your Answer _____

_____

Correct Answers

$$\boxed{911}$$

(B) All of these are appropriate treatment protocols for this patient but your first priority is to ensure an open airway. This patient has probably incurred some upper respiratory burns making an airway important. The question does not state that the patient is still burning; therefore you can begin the cooling process after establishing an airway. In most circumstances this would be done simultaneously, however the airway is the first step. You also want to maintain the patient's body temperature. Burn patients will become hypothermic quickly. Finally, the patient needs to be transported to a hospital that can care for their burns.

Questions

Using the rule of nines, calculate the amount of body surface burned in the patient in the previous question.
(A) 31.5%
(B) 58.5%
(C) 63%
(D) 70%

Your Answer _____

_____

Fast Fact

Pittsburgh's Freedom House paramedics are credited as the first EMT trainees in America. [http://en.wikipedia.org/wiki/Paramedic]

Correct Answers

A–232

(B) When calculating the body surface area that is burned you use the rule of nines. Each leg is 9% for the front and 9% for the back which is 36% for this patient. The arms are 4.5% for the front and 4.5% for the back which is 18% for this patient. The patient has burns to the front of the head. The head is 9% total and therefore this accounts for 4.5% of the BSA burned on this patient for a total of 58.5%.

Questions

911

You are called to the scene of a possible drowning at a local pool. When you arrive on the scene, a bystander is holding the patient at the surface of the water. The patient is unconscious. Your next step is to

(A) begin rescue breathing.
(B) remove the patient from the pool.
(C) start CPR.
(D) apply cervical and spinal immobilization.

Your Answer _____

_____

Career Pulse

EMTs and paramedics have irregular working hours because emergency services function 24 hours a day.

Correct Answers

A–233

911

(D) The best answer for this patient is to apply cervical and spinal immobilization. You do not want to begin rescue breathing since you have not assessed for breathing. The patient is unresponsive but that does not mean they are not breathing. You do not want to remove the patient from the pool until you insure cervical and spinal immobilization. This patient may have struck their head and therefore you need take this precaution.

Questions

You arrive on the scene of a patient who says that she was bitten by fire ants. She has bites all over her legs. Your first step in treating this patient would be to

(A) apply high flow oxygen and remove any jewelry.

(B) cleanse the bites with alcohol to remove the "sting."

(C) transport the patient to the hospital.

(D) use her epi-injector.

Your Answer _____

_____

Correct Answers

A–234

(A) Your first step with this patient is to apply high flow oxygen and remove any jewelry. High flow oxygen should be used on any patient who has suffered a large amount of bites, unless they need ventilatory assistance. Removing jewelry immediately is not necessarily a life-saving measure, however swelling is very common and removing jewelry initially will reduce complications later. You do not want to use the epi pen immediately because you need to make sure that it is the patient's and then call your medical director for permission to assist the patient in administering it to herself. The only symptoms at this time in this scenario are that the patient has been bitten by a large number of fire ants. Therefore, you would want to further assess the patient to see if she is having an allergic reaction to the bites.

Questions

Your patient was stung by a bee. When you assess the sting site, you notice that the stinger is still in the patient's skin. You would

(A) leave the stinger in place.
(B) use a pair of tweezers to remove the stinger.
(C) use a credit card to scrape the stinger off the skin.
(D) use a scalpel and make an "x" incision around the stinger and remove it.

Your Answer _____

_____

Fast Fact

The origins of EMS date back to the days of Napoleon, when the French army utilized horse-drawn "ambulances" to transport the injured soldier from the battlefield. [http://en.wikipedia.org/wiki/Pre-hospital]

Correct Answers

(C)   To remove a stinger that is still in the patient's skin you would use a card, such as a credit card, to scrape the stinger off the skin. The stinger holds the venom and if you use a set of tweezers to remove the stinger, you may actually inject more venom into the patient. Likewise, you do not want to leave the stinger in the patient until you reach the hospital, and at no time should you be making any type of incision with a scalpel on the patient.

Questions

You are called to a home of a 60-year-old male who has been caring for his ill wife for the past year. The patient is very upset and tense. On your assessment you find the patient is diaphoretic, tachycardic, and is breathing rapidly. The patient tells you that he cannot take it any longer. You suspect this patient is suffering from

(A) a phobia of the patient's wife dying.

(B) depression.

(C) acute anxiety.

(D) paranoia.

Your Answer _____

_____

Correct Answers

(C)   This patient exhibits the signs and symptoms of acute anxiety. Granted, he may be fearful his wife may die, but this is typically not a phobia. The same with depression and paranoia. He may be depressed, but his current signs and symptoms exemplify that of an acute anxiety attack. Calming and reassuring the patient is important in this scenario.

Questions

Which of the following is the most common cause
of suicide?
(A) alcohol
(B) drugs
(C) depression
(D) the holidays

Your Answer _____

Which of the following is NOT considered a risk
factor for suicide?
(A) male over the age of 55
(B) strong emotional bonds
(C) family history of suicide
(D) child of an alcoholic parent

Your Answer _____

Correct Answers

A-237

(C) Depression is the most common cause associated with suicide. The other three answers to this question may be factors involved with suicide, but it almost always is in conjunction with depression. There is a myth that most suicides occur around the holidays, this is not true. More suicides occur in the spring of the year than at any other time.

A-238

(B) All of these are risk factors except strong emotional bonds. The lack of strong emotional bonds is a risk factor. Other factors include depression, recent loss of spouse or significant other, chronic debilitating illness, financial set back or loss of job, previous suicide attempt, substance abuse, or mental disorder.

Questions

You are asked to transport a violent patient who needs to be restrained. You would

(A) use soft cushioned restraints.

(B) handcuff the patient to the stretcher.

(C) use plastic ties to secure the patient's hands behind them.

(D) contact your medical director.

Your Answer _____

Fast Fact

Basic Life Support providers are CFRs (Certified First Responders) and EMTs, or EMT-Bs (Emergency Medical Technicians-Basic), and provide all care outlined in the EMS standard of care, except for invasive procedures and (to a certain extent) giving medications. [http://en.wikipedia.org/wiki/Pre-hospital]

Correct Answers

A–239

(D) Restraining a patient is a very sensitive issue and must be handled appropriately. Medical direction needs to be consulted before a patient is restrained. A soft restraint should be used and you should thoroughly document the procedure.

Questions

The normal time span for a pregnancy averages
(A) 12 weeks.
(B) 24 weeks.
(C) 36 weeks.
(D) 40 weeks.

Your Answer _____

Which of the following is typically a result of osteoporosis?
(A) broken bones
(B) kyphosis
(C) calcium deposits
(D) calphosis

Your Answer _____

Correct Answers

A–240

(D) The normal pregnancy time period is usually 40 weeks. It consists of three 3-month periods called trimesters.

A–241

(B) Osteoporosis typically causes kyphosis. This is seen in elderly patients and is identified by the curvature of the spine. Special consideration needs to be taken when immobilizing these patients.

Questions

Q–242

Labor and delivery is broken into three stages. The stage where the placenta is delivered is known as the
(A) third stage.
(B) second stage.
(C) first stage.
(D) none of the above

Your Answer _____

_____

Career Pulse

The make-up of an EMS crew is based upon local resources and the priorities of those who fund the resources.

Correct Answers

A–242

(A) The first stage of labor is when the contractions begin until dilation of the cervix. The second stage begins with the full dilation of the cervix and ends with the delivery of the baby. The third stage begins with the delivery of the baby and ends with the delivery of the placenta.

Questions

A 22-year-old female patient is complaining of abdominal pain and vaginal bleeding. She states that her last menstrual period was two months ago. You would suspect the patient has had a
(A) abruptio placenta.
(B) spontaneous abortion.
(C) uterine rupture.
(D) placenta previa.

Your Answer _____

_____

Fast Fact

EMTs rarely receive training in EKG interpretation, one of the most basic ALS skills. [http:// en.wikipedia.org/wiki/Pre-hospital]

Correct Answers

A–243

(B)   This is symptomatic of a spontaneous abortion. This occurs early in a patient's pregnancy and most often in the first trimester. You need to provide general supportive care and use sanitary pads for the vaginal bleeding. If any clots or products are present, you should take those along to the hospital.

Questions

You are called to a patient in her third trimester of pregnancy. She states she felt a tearing sensation in her lower abdomen that was very painful. There is no bleeding upon your assessment. You would suspect

(A) abruptio placenta.

(B) spontaneous abortion.

(C) uterine rupture.

(D) placenta previa.

Your Answer _____

_____

Career Pulse

There are more than 800,000 EMS providers delivering care in the U.S.

Correct Answers

A–244

(C) This patient has most likely suffered a uterine rupture. This occurs in the third trimester of pregnancy and is symptomatic with a painful tearing sensation. There may or may not be bleeding associated with this. This patient needs to be treated for any signs or symptoms she is exhibiting and receive rapid transport to the hospital.

Questions

You have just delivered a baby boy. The baby is wrapped in a blanket and doing well. You are prepared to cut the umbilical cord. Which of the following is the correct procedure to cut the cord?

(A) Fasten the first clamp four inches from the infant's belly and the second clamp two inches away from the first clamp. Wait until you no longer feel a pulse in the cord and then cut the cord.

(B) Fasten the first clamp two inches from the infant's belly and the second clamp 2 inches away from the first clamp. Wait until you no longer feel a pulse in the cord and then cut the cord.

(C) Fasten the first clamp four inches from the infant's belly and the second clamp four inches away from the first clamp. Wait until you feel a pulse in the cord and then cut the cord.

(D) Fasten the first clamp two inches from the infant's belly and the second clamp four inches away from the first clamp. Wait until you feel a pulse in the cord and then cut the cord.

Your Answer _____

_____

Correct Answers

(A) The proper procedure for cutting the umbilical cord is to fasten the first clamp four inches from the infant's belly and the second clamp two inches away from the first clamp. Wait until you no longer feel a pulse in the cord and then cut the cord between the two clamps.

Questions

In which of the following situations may an EMT-B place their hand in a patient's vagina?
(A) There is never an incident that allows this.
(B) a breech birth
(C) to examine the vagina
(D) to relieve pressure on a prolapsed cord

Your Answer _____

_____

Fast Fact

Advanced Life Support providers are principally paramedics and EMT-Intermediates (EMT-I), who are certified to perform invasive procedures and to give a wide variety of drugs. [http://en.wikipedia.org/wiki/Pre-hospital]

Correct Answers

A-246

(D) The only time an EMT-B is allowed to place their hand in a patient's vagina is when there is a prolapsed cord. This will allow the EMT-B to relieve the pressure off the umbilical cord until the patient can reach the hospital. The presentation of the umbilical cord means that the baby will have to be delivered by cesarean.

Questions

When assessing and treating a geriatric patient, you should address them in the following manner:
(A) By their first name.
(B) By their last name.
(C) By calling them gramps or grandma.
(D) By calling them honey or dear.

Your Answer _____

_____

Career Pulse

In 2000, 64,424 application exams were taken by potential first responders, EMTs, and paramedics. By June of 2005, that number nearly doubled to 112,598 exams taken. The largest increase was for EMTs.

Correct Answers

A–247

(B) When addressing an elderly patient or any patient for that matter it is appropriate to call them by their last name. You may call them by their first name only after you have gained their permission. It is never appropriate to call anyone by a slang name such as hon, honey, sweetie, etc. Also, using the terms grandma and gramps may be offensive to them.

Questions

During the delivery of a baby, you notice a greenish/blackish fluid in the amniotic fluid called meconium. This indicates that

(A) there is blood in the fluid.

(B) this is normal and should be expected.

(C) part of the placenta has detached and is in the fluid.

(D) the baby had a bowel movement while in the uterus.

Your Answer _____

_____

Fast Fact

An essential decision in prehospital care is whether the patient should be immediately taken to the hospital, or advanced care resources taken to the patient where he or she lies. [http://en.wikipedia.org/wiki/Prehospital]

Correct Answers

(D) Meconium is a result of the baby having a bowel movement while in the mother's uterus. This usually occurs as a result of some type of stress placed upon the baby. Airway care is imperative with these deliveries. Be careful not to stimulate the infant prior to getting the nose and mouth suctioned. Aspiration of meconium is fatal in 50% of babies.

Questions

911

Which of the following would you NOT suspect in a patient that has bent the steering wheel in a motor vehicle accident?
(A) fractured pelvis
(B) myocardial contusion
(C) myocardial tamponade
(D) flailed chest

Your Answer _____

911

If a patient is ejected from a vehicle they are _____ more likely to die.
(A) 25 times
(B) 35 times
(C) 50 times
(D) 70 times

Your Answer _____

Correct Answers

A–249

$$\boxed{911}$$

(A) Typically you would not suspect a patient to have a fractured pelvis from hitting the steering wheel. Any type of chest injury should be suspected when a patient hits the steering wheel. It does not mean they have that injury, but the EMT-B should have a high index of suspicion until proven otherwise.

A–250

$$\boxed{911}$$

(A) A patient who is ejected from a vehicle is 25 times more likely to die. It is noted that 10,000 of the 40,000 fatalities from motor vehicle accidents are a result of being ejected from a vehicle. It is also noted that 1 out of 13 victims that are ejected from a vehicle have a spinal fracture.

Questions

Q–251

The right side of the heart has a three-flap valve called the
(A) tri-valve.
(B) seminlunar valve.
(C) mitral valve.
(D) tricuspid valve.

Your Answer _____

Q–252

The normal range of an infants heart rate under the age of 1 is _____.
(A) 140 – 160 beats per minute
(B) 120 – 140 beats per minute
(C) 100 – 120 beats per minute
(D) 80 – 100 beats per minute

Your Answer _____

Correct Answers

A–251

(D) The right side of the heart has a three-flap valve called the tricuspid. The left side of the heart has a two-flap valve called the bicuspid.

A–252

(B) The normal heart rate for a newborn is 140 – 160 beats per minute; for an infant it is 120 – 140 beats per minute; for children 1 – 6 years of age the heart rate is 100 – 120 beats per minute; for children over 6 it is 100 – 120 beats per minute; for adults the rate is 60 – 100 beats per minute and for the elderly, 80 – 100 beats per minute is normal.

Questions

911

Which of the following is a late sign of shock?
(A) hypotension
(B) tachycardia
(C) cyanosis
(D) anxiety

Your Answer _____

911

Which of the following is NOT considered relative
hypovolemic shock?
(A) neurogenic shock
(B) psychogenic shock
(C) hemorrhagic shock
(D) anaphylactic shock

Your Answer _____

Correct Answers

A–253

$$\boxed{911}$$

(A) Patients who suffer from shock will begin by exhibiting signs of anxiety and restlessness due to their hypoxic state. Their pulse will increase in an attempt to compensate. The later sign of shock is hypotension. This is considered uncompensateable shock and the patient at this point is "crashing."

A–254

$$\boxed{911}$$

(C) Relative hypovolemic shock occurs when the blood vessels dilate. There is no loss of blood but the pressure against the vessels decreases because the vessels dilate. Neurogenic shock, psychogenic and anaphylactic shock are all examples of relative hypovolemia. In many instances, such as neurogenic shock, relative hypovolemic shock will happen readily and without warning.

Questions

911

You should never approach a helicopter from the
(A) front.
(B) rear.
(C) left.
(D) right.

Your Answer _____

Career Pulse

*The NREMT (National Registry of Emergency
Medical Technicians) is an informative resource
for the entire EMS community and receives
120,000 telephone calls annually.*

Correct Answers

A–255

$$\boxed{911}$$

(B)   Never approach a helicopter from the rear. The tail rotor is difficult to see. Even if the helicopter is a rear-loading helicopter, approach from the side then go to the rear to load the patient. Always make sure the pilot gives the okay to approach the helicopter.

Questions

911

You are called to the scene of a patient who is in his fifties and being treated for an illness that has been ongoing for the past three weeks. The patient is febrile, diaphoretic, and pale. His blood pressure is 88/40, pulse is 120. You would suspect this patient is suffering from
(A) neurogenic shock.
(B) psychogenic shock.
(C) septic shock.
(D) anaphylactic shock.

Your Answer _____

◄ Fast Fact

The strategy developed for prehospital care in North America is called "Scoop and Run," and is based on the golden-hour concept, i.e., a victim's best chance for survival is in an operating room, with the goal of having the patient in surgery within an hour of the traumatic event. [http://en.wikipedia.org/wiki/Pre-hospital]

Correct Answers

911

(C) Patients who have been sick for periods of time are susceptible to septic shock as a result of infection in the body that causes a vasodilation of the blood vessels. These patients need general supportive care, transport to the hospital for more definitive care and typically need an antibiotic to fight off the infection, before they begin to recover.

Questions

911

You are applying direct pressure to a 12-year-old female's lower leg which was lacerated by a large piece of glass. The bleeding continues to soak through the bandages even while applying direct pressure. Your next step would be to

(A) elevate the extremity.

(B) apply pressure at the femoral artery.

(C) apply a tourniquet.

(D) remove the blood soaked bandages and replace with clean bandages.

Your Answer _____

_____

Career Pulse

As nursing shortages in the U.S. become more and more prevalent, paramedics are being increasingly used in Emergency Departments and Intensive Care Units of hospitals. Often paramedics operate with greater latitude and autonomy than many nurses. [http://en.wikipedia.org/wiki/Paramedic]

Correct Answers

$$\boxed{911}$$

(A) If blood continues to soak through your pressure dressing, your next step would be to elevate the extremity. If the bleeding still does not stop, apply pressure to her pulse point, which in this case would be the femoral artery.

Questions

911

Which of the following is NOT a contraindication of applying and inflating the MAST garment?
(A) objects impaled in a site that would be covered with the garment
(B) the last three months of pregnancy
(C) pelvic and femur fracture
(D) pulmonary edema

Your Answer _____

911

You would expect the exit wound from a gunshot to be
(A) larger than the entrance.
(B) smaller than the entrance.
(C) the same size as the entrance.
(D) You would not expect to see an exit wound.

Your Answer _____

Correct Answers

A–258

911

(C) The MAST pants are not used to the extent they once were, but are still used to stabilize femur and pelvic fractures. The only true contraindication of the MAST is pulmonary edema. However you should not apply and inflate over an impaled object and you should avoid use in the last three months of pregnancy.

A–259

911

(A) Typically the exit of a gunshot wound is larger than the entrance. In some instances, you will not see an exit wound if the bullet becomes lodged in the body but you should always look for an exit wound.

Questions

$$\boxed{911}$$

You arrive on the scene of patient who has amputated his arm at the elbow. Which of the following best describes the way you should transport the extremity?

(A) Packed on ice.

(B) Wrapped in sterile dressings and kept cool with ice.

(C) Placed in a plastic bag without any ice.

(D Soaked in sterile water and placed in a plastic bag.

Your Answer _____

_____

Fast Fact

Pioneering advances in telemedicine, including the use of videocameras, now make it possible for advanced medical direction and advice to be supplied to emergency medical technicians, military medics, and nurses or other community health care providers in remote or isolated areas or even aboard cruise ships. [http://en.wikipedia.org/wiki/Pre-hospital]

Correct Answers

$\boxed{911}$

(B)　An amputated part needs to be handled very carefully. The part should be wrapped in a sterile dressing and kept cool but never placed directly on ice. The care the amputated part receives, coupled with the time the patient arrives at the hospital, are critical components of a successful reattachment.

Questions

911

You are called to the scene of a possible stabbing. The patient has a large laceration to his abdomen and his abdominal organs are protruding. This is called a/an

(A) abdominal protrusion.

(B) ruptured abdomen.

(C) abdominal content displacement.

(D) abdominal evisceration.

Your Answer _____

_____

Career Pulse

Paramedics are often used as chief medical personnel on offshore drilling platforms and on MEDEVACs and airplanes. [http://en.wikipedia.org/wiki/Paramedic]

Correct Answers

$$\boxed{911}$$

(D) This type of injury is called an abdominal evisceration.

Questions

911

You treat the patient in the previous question by
- (A) pushing the abdominal contents back in and covering with dry sterile dressings.
- (B) pushing the abdominal contents back in and covering with moist sterile dressings.
- (C) not pushing the abdominal contents back in and covering with moist sterile dressings.
- (D) not pushing the abdominal contents back in and not covering with any dressings.

Your Answer _____

_____

Fast Fact

The goal of EMT intervention is to rapidly evaluate a patient's condition and to maintain a patient's airway, breathing and circulation by CPR and defibrillation. Also, to control external bleeding, prevent shock, and prevent further injury or disability by immobilizing potential spinal or other bone fractures, while expediting the safe and timely transport of the patient to a hospital emergency department for definitive medical care. [http://en.wikipedia.org/wiki/Emergency_ medical_technician]

Correct Answers

$$\boxed{911}$$

(C)   You should not push the abdominal contents back in which may cause further damage. It is important to prevent further contamination and injury and also important that contents not be allowed to dry out; therefore, a dry sterile dressing soaked with sterile water is recommended. This patient will need immediate surgical intervention.

Questions

911

Your patient has a large opening to the neck as a result of a traumatic injury. A complication of leaving this injury open and administering proper treatment is
(A) skin necrosis.
(B) pneumothorax.
(C) neurogenic shock.
(D) pulmonary embolism.

Your Answer _____

_____

Career Pulse

Paramedics may be employed in many different medical fields that do not necessarily involve transportation of patients. Such positions may include phlebotomy, blood banks, research labs and educational fields.
[http://en.wikipedia.org/wiki/Paramedic]

Correct Answers

$$\boxed{911}$$

(D) If a large neck wound is left open and untreated, the patient may develop a pulmonary embolism which occurs by air being sucked into the vessels. A large wound to the neck should be covered and sealed similar to the treatment for a sucking chest wound.

Questions

911

You arrive on the scene of patient who has impaled her foot on a typewriter. The patient states she jumped from the top bunk and did not see it on the floor below. She does not want to go to the hospital because she is embarrassed. You should

(A) not remove the typewriter and transport her to the hospital.

(B) remove the typewriter and transport her to the hospital.

(C) remove the typewriter and not transport her to the hospital.

(D) not remove the typewriter and not transport her to the hospital.

Your Answer _____

_____

Correct Answers

$$\boxed{911}$$

(A) An impaled object should never be removed unless it is occluding the airway. The patient needs to be transported to the hospital and then have the object removed. If the object is attached to a larger object, disassemble the object and take the patient and the smaller portion of the object to the hospital. If cutting a metal object, you need to take care so as not to produce an amount of heat that will harm the patient as a result of friction. Place your hand on the object between where you are cutting and the patient to monitor the heat being generated.

Questions

Your patient has suffered an injury to the left ankle. Later you find out from the ER doctor that the patient injured their ligaments by overstretching and partially tearing them. This type of injury is called a

(A) strain.
(B) sprain.
(C) fracture.
(D) muscle pull.

Your Answer _____

_____

Fast Fact

EMTs and paramedics of the New York City Fire Department's Emergency Medical Service Command, along with hospital-employed EMTs and paramedics under its jurisdiction, respond to more than 3,000 requests for 9-1-1 assistance daily; over 1.3 million calls annually (2003). [http://en.wikipedia.org/wiki/ Emergency_medical_technician]

Correct Answers

A–265

(B) This type of injury is a sprain. It is difficult to assess the difference between a sprain, strain, and sometimes a fracture in the field. All are treated the same in the pre-hospital setting. A strain is a soft-tissue injury or muscle spasm that occurs around a joint anywhere in the musculature. A fracture is a break in the bone.

Questions

Which of the following is the most appropriate pre-hospital treatment for the patient in the previous question?

(A) Apply traction and ice and keep the limb lower than the rest of the body.

(B) Apply traction and heat and elevate the limb.

(C) Splint the ankle, apply heat, and elevate.

(D) Splint the ankle, apply ice, and elevate.

Your Answer _____

Correct Answers

A–266

(D) A sprain, strain, or fracture are all treated the same in the pre-hospital environment since it is difficult to distinguish between the three. Immobilize the extremity with a splint and apply ice. Also, elevate the extremity which will help to reduce swelling and possible further damage.

Questions

911

Your patient dislocated her left shoulder when she fell. The proper procedure for immobilizing a dislocated shoulder is to
(A) splint her left arm to the left side of her body.
(B) attempt to reset the dislocation.
(C) apply a sling and swathe to immobilize the left arm and shoulder.
(D) apply a rigid splint to the front and back of the shoulder to immobilize.

Your Answer _____

Correct Answers

911

(C)   The proper way to immobilize a shoulder dislocation is to sling and swathe the affected arm and shoulder. Do not attempt to reset a shoulder dislocation. There are a number of complications associated with attempting to reset a dislocation. If there is not a distal pulse in the extremity affected by a dislocation, gentle traction can be applied. You should also not delay transport for these patients.

Questions

911

You are treating a patient with a fractured femur.
The most appropriate splint to use for this patient
would be
(A) a ladder splint.
(B) the other leg.
(C) two board splints.
(D) a traction splint.

Your Answer _____

Career Pulse

*The biggest difference between EMT-I's
and Paramedics is that while EMT-I's handle
advanced airway management like Paramedics,
they do not have as in-depth cardiac training
and usually administer fewer medications.
[http://en.wikipedia.org/wiki/Pre-hospital]*

Correct Answers

911

(D)   A traction splint is used for femur fractures. Ladder splints are used for angulated fractures. Board splints are good to use for extremity fractures, however, on the leg they should be used primarily for splinting lower leg injuries or hip dislocations and fractures. You can always use the other leg when you have no other splinting options available, but in this scenario a traction splint is the best choice.

Questions

You have immobilized your patient's arm with a board splint. The patient had a radial pulse before applying the splint. After you finish, you assess the pulse at the radial and cannot detect one. The most likely cause of this is:

(A) The fracture compressing the artery.
(B) This should be expected when splinting a patient.
(C) The extremity should be elevated.
(D) The splint may be applied too tightly.

Your Answer _____

Correct Answers

A–269

(D) The most likely cause of the patient not having a distal pulse is that the splint was applied too tightly. This is indicated by the fact that the patient had a distal pulse prior to the application of the splint. The fact that the fracture compressing the artery may indeed be what is happening, but it is most likely due to the splint application. You should loosen the ties on the splint and reassess the patient's PMS.

Questions

$$911$$

The patient you are treating has suffered a blow to the back of the head. The most likely area of the brain affected would be the

(A) occipital region.
(B) parietal region.
(C) temporal region.
(D) frontal region.

Your Answer _____

_____

Fast Fact

Wilderness first aid is the provision of first aid under conditions where the evacuation of an injured person may be delayed due to constraints of terrain, weather, and available equipment. It may be necessary to care for an injured person for several hours or days. [http://en.wikipedia.org/wiki/Wilderness_first_aid]

Correct Answers

911

(A) The occipital region is located in the back of the skull and is the most likely region affected by a blow to the back of the head.

Questions

$\boxed{911}$

A witness tells you that the patient was responsive immediately after being struck in the head with a baseball, but is now unconscious. The right pupil is fixed and dilated. The bystander tells you the patient was struck on the right side of the head. The patient is most likely suffering from

(A) intracranial bleeding.

(B) subdural hematoma.

(C) basilar skull fracture.

(D) epidural hematoma.

Your Answer _____

Correct Answers

$$\boxed{911}$$

(B) These are classic signs of a subdural hematoma. Patients who have subdural hematomas present with deterioration in level of consciousness, dilation of one pupil, abnormal respirations, rising blood pressure, and slowing pulse. Epidural hematoma patients lose consciousness, regain consciousness and then go unresponsive. They also typically complain of a severe headache and commonly seize.

Questions

911

Which of the following are the signs of Cushing's triad?

(A) increased pulse, increased blood pressure, change in respiratory rate

(B) decreased pulse, increased blood pressure, change in respiratory rate

(C) increased pulse, decreased blood pressure, change in respiratory rate

(D) decreased pulse, decreased blood pressure, change in respiratory rate

Your Answer _____

_____

Career Pulse

EMTs are trained in basic medical knowledge and skills. [http://en.wikipedia.org/wiki/Emergency_medical_technician]

Correct Answers

$$\boxed{911}$$

(B) Cushing's triad is indicative of a closed head injury with increased intracranial pressure (ICP). Therefore, the signs would be an increase in blood pressure, a decrease in pulse rate and a change in respiratory rate. When ICP increases, the vagus nerve is stimulated and reduces the pulse rate. These are also late signs in patients with a head injury.

Questions

$\boxed{911}$

In patients with closed head injuries, a respiratory pattern called Cheyne-Stokes breathing occurs. This pattern is best described as:

(A) rapid breathing then shallow breathing

(B) slow and shallow breathing with periods of apnea and then to deep breathing

(C) slow and shallow breathing then deep ventilation then back to slow and shallow breathing followed by a period of apnea

(D) rapid breathing with periods of apnea

Your Answer _____

Correct Answers

$$\boxed{911}$$

(C) Cheyne–Stokes breathing is when the respiratory pattern of a patient goes from slow and shallow breathing to a deep ventilation and back again to slow and shallow breathing followed by a period of apnea.

Questions

$$\boxed{911}$$

There are levels of posturing that occur in patients with head injuries known as decorticate and decerebrate posturing. Which of the following statements is correct?

(A) Decorticate posturing happens in the later stages of a head injury and decerebrate posturing happens in the early stages.

(B) Decorticate posturing is when the patient's arms are drawn to the body and decerebrate posturing is when the arms are positioned away from the body.

(C) Decorticate posturing is when the patient's arms are positioned away from the body and decerebrate posturing is when the patient's arms are drawn to the body.

(D) Decorticate and decerebrate posturing is not indicative of a head injury and none of the above are correct.

Your Answer _____

_____

Correct Answers

$$\boxed{911}$$

(B) Closed head injury patients will progressively decrease their responsiveness. The patient will initially withdraw from painful stimulus. Later the patient will present with decorticate posturing which is when the patient draws their arms to the core of their body and the lower extremities become rigid and extended. The late signs of a closed head injury is when the patient exhibits decerebrate posturing which is when the patient's lower and upper extremities become rigid and extend away from the body. At this point the effects are usually irreversible.

Questions

911

You are treating a patient who has a possible spinal injury. The patient states that he cannot move his extremities from his waist down. This is referred to as

(A) hemiplegia.
(B) quadriplegia.
(C) paraplegia.
(D) pelaplegia.

Your Answer _____

_____

Correct Answers

$$\boxed{911}$$

(C) Paralysis from the waist down is called paraplegia while paralysis from the neck down is called quadriplegia. Paralysis on one side of the body is called hemiplegia.

Questions

$$\boxed{911}$$

You are called to a high school football game. A 14-year-old male is lying on the ground complaining of neck and back pain. He was wearing a helmet and shoulder pads with all the protective equipment while playing. You notice the helmet does not fit tightly. The appropriate care for this patient is to

(A) remove the helmet and leave the other protective gear on.

(B) leave the protective gear on and immobilize.

(C) remove the helmet and shoulder pads.

(D) leave the helmet on but remove the rest of the protective gear and immobilize.

Your Answer _____

Correct Answers

$$\boxed{911}$$

(C) High school football players do not always have the best equipment. In this situation the helmet does not fit tightly and may cause more harm than good. It is appropriate to remove the helmet and shoulder pads of this patient. Any time you remove a helmet, you must remove the shoulder pads. Likewise most instances require you to remove motorcycle helmets. They typically create a problem in immobilizing a patient on a backboard, plus it is difficult to manage the airway with full face shield helmets.

Questions

911

Which device would you use to immobilize a patient when extricating them from a vehicle?
(A) K.E.D.
(B) long spine board
(C) scoop board
(D) rapid extrication

Your Answer _____

_____

Fast Fact

Triage is a system used by medical or emergency personnel to ration limited medical resources when the number of injured needing care exceeds the resources available to perform care. The objective: to treat the greatest number of patients possible.
[http://en.wikipedia.org/wiki/Triage]

Correct Answers

A–277

$$\boxed{911}$$

(A) A K.E.D. is a Kendrick Extrication Device used to extricate a patient from a vehicle. A rapid extrication is a procedure performed when the patient's life is in jeopardy and you need to get the patient out of the vehicle immediately. During a rapid extrication the patient is extricated directly from the vehicle on to the long board. There are risks associated with taking this short cut and should only be done when the patient's life is in jeopardy.

Questions

You arrive on the scene of a 12-year-old female who is seizing. The school nurse tells you that this is the patient's third seizure and the patient has not regained consciousness between seizures. This is known as

(A) aura.
(B) postictal.
(C) epilepsy.
(D) status epilepticus.

Your Answer _____

Correct Answers

(D) An aura is what occurs before a patient has a seizure. A smell or sense indicates to the patient that they are going to seize. Postictal is the period after one has seized. The patient is usually lethargic and sleepy, but will regain full consciousness usually within 30 minutes. Epilepsy is defined as two or more seizures that are unprovoked. The example in this question is representative of status epilepticus where the patient does not regain consciousness between the seizures.

Questions

You are responding to an emergency call. You have your lights and siren on. Your lights and siren allow you to

(A) exceed the posted speed limit as fast you can go.
(B) disregard all traffic laws.
(C) have the right away at all times.
(D) proceed through red lights and stop signs with due regard after you assure that it is safe to do so.

Your Answer _____

_____

Correct Answers

A–279

(D) Most states allow emergency vehicles to exceed posted speed limits and ignore various signals, etc. However, as a driver of an emergency vehicle you need to operate it in a safe manner. Even though you can ignore certain traffic signs and procedures, you are still held accountable for your actions and in most instances you are held to a higher standard.

Questions

You are responding to the scene of a truck fire for standby. You are the first unit to arrive on the scene. You should
(A) go directly to the truck to see what is burning.
(B) stage your vehicle upwind and try to identify any placards.
(C) stage your vehicle downwind and attempt to identify any placards.
(D) attempt to make a rescue of the driver from the vehicle.

Your Answer _____

_____

Correct Answers

A–280

(B) A truck may be carrying a number of items. Until you can identify that the scene is safe you should not approach. It is appropriate to stay upwind out of the path of the smoke and use a pair of binoculars to attempt to identify placards on the vehicle. Scene safety is a priority and you should not attempt to make rescue. Even if the fire department is responding, it is still a great idea to attempt to identify any placards from a distance. This will aid the fire department in their attempt to extinguish the fire and also be helpful if they should approach the scene.

Questions

911

You arrive at the scene of a mass casualty incident involving 12 patients. Which of the following patients would you classify as the highest priority?

(A) a 37-year-old male with multiple bone fractures

(B) an 18-year-old female in cardiac arrest

(C) a 58-year-old male with uncontrolled bleeding and shortness of breath

(D) an 8-year-old female with burns to both of her feet

Your Answer _____

_____

Correct Answers

$$\boxed{911}$$

(C) Triaging is a difficult event for an EMT-B at the scene of an MCI. An EMT-B will sometimes make the hardest decisions of their life, because they have to decide who to treat and who not to resuscitate. In most instances the EMT-B will only deal with one patient and will make every effort to save that person's life. At the scene of an MCI, you cannot do that and need to make tough choices. The 18-year-old is in cardiac arrest and would be classified as a low priority. The patient with multiple bone fractures and the child with burns would be classified as a moderate priority. The patient short of breath, with uncontrolled bleeding, would be the highest priority in this scenario and should be treated first.

Questions

911

A mass casualty incident is considered to occur when

(A) your resources are outnumbered by your patients.

(B) there are three or more patients.

(C) there are six or more patients.

(D) there are more patients than ambulances on the scene.

Your Answer _____

Career Pulse

Many firefighters and some police officers (particularly in the highway patrol) are now also cross-trained as EMTs. [http://en.wikipedia. org/wiki/Emergency_medical_technician]

Correct Answers

$$\boxed{911}$$

(A) A mass casualty occurs when there are more patients than there are resources. You could say more patients than ambulances, however this is not the best answer. Keep in mind you may have two patients and one ambulance, or there may be additional units responding to the incident, but this does not make it a mass casualty. In many organizations, an EMS crew may transport two patients in one ambulance. There is no magic number for an MCI. In New York City it takes a greater incident than an incident in rural Wyoming where there may only be one ambulance within 100 miles.

Questions

$$\boxed{911}$$

You arrive on the scene of a 20-year-old male lying on the ground. Upon examination you notice blood soaked through his shirt. When his shirt is removed there is frothy blood at the opening of the wound and a sucking sound is heard. Your initial reaction would be to

(A) place your gloved hand over the wound.

(B) place your hand over the wound.

(C) apply an occlusive dressing.

(D) apply a sterile dressing.

Your Answer _____

Correct Answers

911

(A) This is indicative of a sucking chest wound and you should immediately place your gloved hand on the wound and seal it. An occlusive dressing can be placed on the wound next. Never place an ungloved hand on a patient who is bleeding or any body substance that could transmit an infectious disease.

Questions

You have just completed a call and need to clean your unit, including the stretcher. You note that there is blood on the lift rails of the stretcher. The most appropriate cleaning solution would be

(A) use undiluted bleach.

(B) a 1:100 solution of bleach to water.

(C) a 1:10 solution of bleach to water.

(D) a 1:1 solution of bleach to water.

Your Answer _____

Correct Answers

A–284

(C)   A lot is not always better. You should never use an undiluted concentration of bleach on your unit or equipment. The proper solution is 1:10, 1 part bleach to 10 parts of water. At this concentration it will adequately kill most bacteria, viruses, and fungi. There are commercial products on the market for disinfecting also. Read the label to make sure it will do what you want, before you use it.

Questions

911

You arrive on the scene of a motor vehicle accident. The vehicle is resting on its side and the patient is still in the vehicle. Your first action would be to

(A) establish an airway.
(B) crib the vehicle using edges and boards.
(C) have the patient get out of the vehicle.
(D) place flares around the vehicle to secure the area.

Your Answer _____

_____

Correct Answers

911

(B) A vehicle that is resting on its side is very unstable. The first thing an EMT-B should do is stabilize the vehicle. This is accomplished by placing wedges and boards to secure the vehicle from rolling over. If you do not have cribbing on your unit, wait for a unit that does. Never have a patient self-extricate themselves from a vehicle. It is never a good idea to use flares at the scene of a motor vehicle accident. If the vehicle is leaking fuel, it may cause a fire.

Questions

911

When working at the scene of a hazardous materials incident you are required to wear a fully encapsulated suit. This level of protection would be classified as
(A) Level D.
(B) Level C.
(C) Level B.
(D) Level A.

Your Answer _____

_____

Fast Fact

Simple triage is used at the scene of a mass casualty incident to choose patients who require immediate transport to the hospital to save their lives as opposed to patients who can wait for help later. [http://en.wikipedia.org/wiki/Triage]

Correct Answers

911

(D) A fully encapsulated suit is the highest level of protection at the scene of a hazardous material incident. This suit is classified as a Level A suit. Level D protection is considered your work uniform. Level C is protective gear that firefighters wear, and Level B is a chemical suit. All levels of protection have respiratory protection except for Level D.

Questions

911

You are trained to the level of hazardous material first responder. At this level of training, you should never enter
(A) any zone.
(B) the cold zone or higher.
(C) the warm zone or higher.
(D) the hot zone.

Your Answer _____

_____

Correct Answers

$$\boxed{911}$$

(D) An EMT-B who is trained at the first responder level may enter the cold and warm zones. The only individuals who should be entering the hot zone must be trained at least to the hazardous material technician level.

Questions

911

You arrive at the scene of a possible unconscious patient located in a lab setting. On the exterior of the room there is a NFPA diamond with a 4 in the blue portion of the diamond. This indicates an
(A) extreme health hazard.
(B) extreme fire hazard.
(C) extreme reactivity hazard.
(D) extreme water reactivity.

Your Answer _____

_____

Correct Answers

$$\boxed{911}$$

(A) The NFPA diamond has four diamonds inside the main diamond. The blue diamond represents health hazard. The red diamond is fire and the yellow diamond represents reactivity. The white diamond at the bottom represents special considerations. The numbering system goes from 0 – 4. The number 4 represents extreme. These are typically found at fixed locations such as a lab.

Questions

911

You are at the scene of a mass casualty incident. Who is in charge of the overall scene?

(A) the EMT-B
(B) the incident commander
(C) the paramedic
(D) the medical director

Your Answer _____

_____

Career Pulse

Patient treatment guidelines are described in protocols following both national guidelines and local medical policies. [http://en.wikipedia. org/wiki/Emergency_medical_technician]

Correct Answers

$$\boxed{911}$$

(B) An incident management system (IMS) is used at major events such as a mass casualty incident. The incident commander is in charge of the scene, and can be anyone with any level of certification. They are the main contact or focal point to coordinate the efforts of all who are involved. In many instances involving mass casualties, unless you have an abundance of paramedics and physicians, you would not want these individuals to be the incident commander. Rather, you want these individuals treating the patients.

Questions

Which of the following is NOT a risk factor for a stroke?
(A) previous TIA
(B) diabetes
(C) hypervolemia
(D) hypertension

Your Answer _____

During your assessment you find a possible fractured leg and hear the bones grinding together. This is called
(A) crepitus.
(B) complete fracture.
(C) subcutaneous fracture.
(D) multi-linear fracture.

Your Answer _____

Correct Answers

A-290

(C) The risk factors for stroke include hypertension, cigarette smoking, cardiovascular disease, diabetes, and previous TIAs.

A-291

(A) Crepitus is the sound that two bone ends make when they grind together. This is a result of a fracture.

Questions

911

You are at the scene of a mass casualty incident involving at least 18 patients. There needs to be
(A) a patient care report completed only on those patients wanting transport.
(B) a patient care report completed only on those patients that are treated.
(C) a patient care report completed on all patients.
(D) no patient care report on any of the patients since it is a mass casualty.

Your Answer _____

_____

Correct Answers

$$\boxed{911}$$

(C) A mass casualty is no different from any other call when it comes to paperwork. Every patient whether dead or alive, treated or not treated, transported or not transported, needs a patient care report completed for them. If they refuse treatment and/or transport, they still need to sign the refusal form.

Questions

Your patient was bitten by a brown recluse spider. These bites result in a
(A) local injury.
(B) systemic injury.
(C) peripheral injury.
(D) general injury.

Your Answer _____

An intubated adult patient should be ventilated every
(A) 3 to 5 seconds.
(B) 4 to 6 seconds.
(C) 5 to 7 seconds.
(D) 6 to 8 seconds.

Your Answer _____

Correct Answers

A–293

(A) Brown recluse spider bites cause a local injury. Within 7-14 days the bite develops into an open sore. A black widow spider bite, on the other hand, is a more systemic injury.

A–294

(D) An intubated adult patient should be ventilated every six to eight seconds.

Questions

Q-295

$$\boxed{911}$$

You arrive on the scene of a 16-year-old female patient sitting at the bottom of a cistern (a hole in the ground that is used to collect water). The patient does not answer your voice and appears unconscious. Your next step would be to

(A) climb into the hole and begin resuscitation efforts.

(B) use respiratory protection such as an SCBA and enter the hole.

(C) climb into the hole and remove the patient.

(D) attempt a rescue any way you can to get her out.

Your Answer _____

_____

Correct Answers

$$\boxed{911}$$

(B) You never want to enter an environment that is unsafe. Typically holes in the ground are low in oxygen and may have harmful gases. There have been rescuers who have died entering holes in the ground trying to save a patient. Always wear protective equipment, including respiratory protection, when entering a confined space. If you do not have the equipment and/or are not trained to use the equipment, then you should wait for other rescuers who are able to perform such duties.

Questions

911

You are requesting helicopter transport for a patient who was involved in a motor vehicle accident. It is 2 a.m. The minimum area you need to mark off for a night time landing is

(A) 60 feet × 60 feet.
(B) 100 feet × 100 feet.
(C) 160 feet × 160 feet.
(D) 200 feet × 200 feet.

Your Answer _____

_____

Correct Answers

911

(B) The typical area that you need to mark off for a night time landing pad for a helicopter is 100 feet by 100 feet. During the day it is 60 feet by 60 feet. Keep in mind your local medical helicopter service may have different standards, however these are the recognized guidelines for helicopter landing zones.

Questions

911

You are the first unit on the scene of a mass casualty incident. Your responsibility is to
(A) treat the first patient with life-threatening injury.
(B) begin removing the patients from the scene.
(C) establish a treatment area.
(D) begin triaging patients.

Your Answer _____

Correct Answers

A–297

$$\boxed{911}$$

(D) The first unit on the scene of a mass casualty incident typically begins triaging patients to identify those with life-threatening injuries. Later arriving units will set up the sectors including treatment and transportation. Triage is very difficult because you have to make life and death decisions for each patient you come in contact with.

Questions

You have just intubated a patient in cardiac arrest. Your partner tells you he hears breath sounds on the right side, but not on the left. You would suspect that you

(A) intubated the right stem bronchus.
(B) intubated the left stem bronchus
(C) are in the proper position.
(D) are in the esophagus.

Your Answer _____

Career Pulse

Some large companies, especially industrial facilities, maintain their own in-house EMTs as part of the plant's firefighting or security guard force. [http://en.wikipedia.org/wiki/Emergency_ medical_technician]

Correct Answers

A–298

(A) If you hear breath sounds on the right side of the chest, but not on the left, chances are you intubated the right stem bronchus. Deflate the cuff and move the tube back slightly and re-evaluate.

Questions

911

You are attempting to intubate a patient. The vocal cords appear to be anterior and you are having a difficult time visualizing them. You could
(A) have your partner try.
(B) ask your partner to perform the Sellick maneuver.
(C) insert the laryngoscope in further.
(D) wait until you get to the hospital.

Your Answer _____

_____

Correct Answers

911

(B) Using the Sellick maneuver in this patient will help make the cords more visible. The Sellick maneuver or cricoid pressure also helps reduce the chances of the patient vomiting during intubation.

Questions

911

The best way to confirm endotracheal tube placement is to
(A) listen to breath sounds.
(B) watch for chest rise and fall.
(C) visualize the tube passing through the cords.
(D) assess skin color.

Your Answer _____

_____

Correct Answers

$$\boxed{911}$$

(C)   There is no better way to confirm tube placement than watching the ET tube pass through the
vocal cords. The other measures are also important means to document tube placement, including
watching the chest rise and fall, making sure the
abdomen does not rise, and checking for breath
sounds over both lung fields and the epigastrium.
Using commercial products to check the tube can
also be appropriate. CO detectors are part of a bag-
valve-mask and are also helpful indicators.

Blank Cards for
Your Own Questions

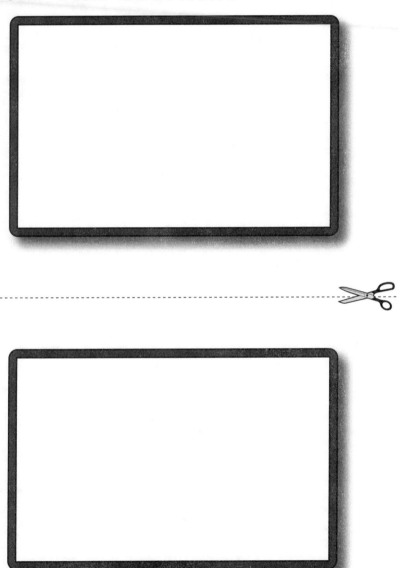

Correct Answers

Blank Cards for
Your Own Questions

Correct Answers

Blank Cards for
Your Own Questions

Correct Answers

Blank Cards for
Your Own Questions

Correct Answers

Blank Cards for
Your Own Questions

Correct Answers

Blank Cards for
Your Own Questions

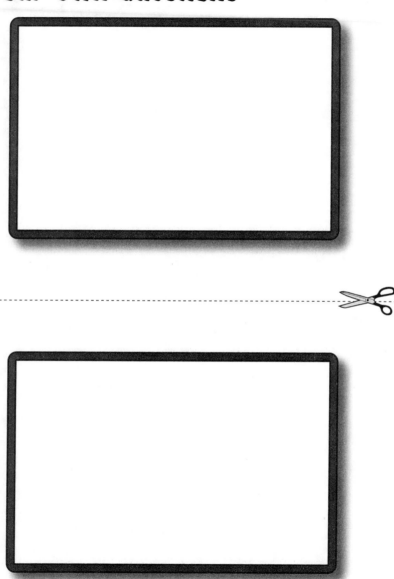

Correct Answers

INDEX

Note: Numbers in the Index refer to question numbers.

Abandonment of patient, 14
Abdomen
  evisceration of, 261, 262
  internal bleeding of, 109
  trauma to, 8
Abortion, spontaneous, 243
Activated charcoal poisoning, 191, 222
Acute anxiety attack, 236
AED, use of, 8, 200, 203
Air embolism, 95
Airway obstruction, 30, 195
Albuterol, 193
Alcohol consumption, 69
Allergic reactions, treatment of, 70,
  190. See also Anaphylactic shock
Amputation
  of arm, 260
  treatment for, 114, 260
Anaphylactic shock, 68, 218
Aneurysm, 186
Angina pectoris, 6, 201, 202
Anxiety attack, acute, 236
Arm
  amputation at elbow, 260
  bones of, 162
Asthma, assessment of, 172
Autonomic nervous system, 124
Avulsion, 111
Back injury. See Neck and back injury
Basilar skull fracture, 122
Battery, liabilities associated with, 160
Bicuspid valve, 3
Bleeding, treatment of, 106, 107, 257.
  See also Clotting
Blood, flow of, 2
Blood pressure, assessment of, 168
Brain, trauma to, 270
Burns, 225, 227

calculation of burnt surface, 232
from electrical source, 117
full thickness, 229, 231
types of, 115, 116
Capillary refill, 41
Carbon monoxide poisoning, 74–76
Cardiac arrest, 147, 210
Cardiovascular disorders
  AED, use of, 200, 202
  angina pectoris, 6, 201, 203
  cardiac arrest, 147, 210
  cardiogenic shock, 207
  congestive heart failure, 205, 206
  intubation in, 298
  myocardial infarction, 6, 204
  nitroglycerin, administration of,
    208, 209
  symptoms of, 1
Chest compression, 144, 145, 211, 212,
  214
Chest injuries
  from motor vehicle accidents, 249,
    250
  with sucking sounds, 283
Chest pain, mnemonics in assessment
  of, 42, 45
Cheyne-Stokes breathing, 273
Child abuse, 150
Choking, 20, 146
  pediatric patients, treatment of, 136
Clotting, 165. See also Bleeding
Cold injuries. See Frostbite; Localized
  cold injuries
Conduction, heat transfer by, 85, 224
Confidentiality of patient information,
  15, 187
Congestive heart failure, 205, 206
Consciousness, level of, 28, 183. See
  also Unconsciousness
Convection, heat transfer by, 86
COPD patients, hypoxic drive in, 59
Crepitus, 291
Croup, 199
Cushing's triad, 272

Death. *See also* Terminal illness
  grieving process, 156
  likelihood of, in motor vehicle
    accidents, 250
Decontamination, 153
Decorticate and decerebrate posturing,
    and head injury, 274
Delivery. *See also* Labor; Pregnancy
  meconium, 248
  umbilical cord, 245, 246
Depression, 96
Diabetes, 61
  treatment of, 192
  Type II, 217
Disinfection, 148, 284
Dislocation
  of hip, 138
  immobilization of joint, 267
  of shoulder, 121, 267
Drowning, 233
Drug overdose, 48, 79, 80, 224
Electrical burns, 117
Emergency move, 173
Emphysema, 57
EMT-B
  emergency call, response to, 279
  functions, primary, 151
  medication, assistance with, 50
  scene assessment, 155
  scope of practice of, 152
  stress management, 158
  stress, response to, 157
Endotracheal tube placement, 300
Epidural hematoma, 123
Epiglottitis, 137
Epistaxis, 108
Esophageal varices, 84
Evisceration of abdomen, 261, 262
Extremities, assessment of, 36
Eye injury, treatment of, 125, 129
Falls, 25
  assessment of, 34, 35
Femur, fracture of, 268, 269
Flailed segment of rib, 35

Fractures
  crepitus, 291
  of leg, 268, 291
  MAST garment, use of, 258
  of skull, 122
  splinting of, 269
Frostbite, 220, 228. *See also* Localized
  cold injuries
Gall bladder, rupture of, 82
Geriatric patients
  assessment of, 46, 48
  form of address, 247
Gunshot wounds, 259

Hazardous material
  exposure to, 77, 78
  NFPA diamond, indicator of hazard,
    288
  protective gear, types of, 286
  radioactive incident, 141
  training, level of, 287
Head injury
  and brain trauma, 270
  and Cheyne-Stokes breathing, 273
  Cushing's triad, 272
  and posturing, levels of, 274
  subdural hematoma, 271
Heart, tricuspid valve, 251
Heat stroke, 89, 223
  treatment of, 90
Hemorrhagic stroke, 63
Hepatitis, 154
Hip, dislocation of, 138
History of patient, 32, 38, 169
Hollow organs, 82
Hyperglycemia, 17
Hyperventilation, 198
Hypoglycemia, 216
Hypotension, 253
Hypothermia, treatment of, 87
Hypovolemic shock, 128, 254
Hypoxic drive, 59
Immune system, 5
Impaled objects, treatment for, 112
Infants
  heart rates of, 252

respiratory rate, normal, 31
Infectious diseases, prevention of, 9
Insect bites
    injury, types of, 293
    treatment of, 234, 235
Insulin production, 215
Intubation
    of cardiac patients, 298
    endotracheal tube placement, 300
    Sellick maneuver in, 299
    ventilation with, 294
Kidneys, 64
Labor, 103, 104. *See also* Delivery;
    Pregnancy
    first stage of, 242
    prolapsed cord, 246
    second stage of, 97
Liability, 14, 182
    battery and, 160
    laws, types of, 159
Ligaments, 119
Localized cold injuries, treatment of,
    88. *See also* Frostbite
Marine life, sting or bite by, 93
Mass casualty incident
    definition of, 282
    incident command system, 142, 289
    patient care report for, 292
    responsibilities of EMT-B, 297
    treatment priority at, 143, 281
MAST garments, 258
Mechanism of injury, 33
Meconium, 248
Mnemonics
    in chest pain assessment, 42, 45
    in extremities assessment, 36
Motor vehicle accident
    actions taken at, 27
    air transportation of patients, 296
    chest injuries from, 249
    death, likelihood of, 250
    extrication procedures, 277
    incident command system, 142, 289
    stabilizing vehicle, 285
Musculoskeletal system, 118

Myocardial infarction, 6, 204
Nasopharyngeal airway, 178
Neck and back injury, 94, 276
    open, 113
Newborns, respiratory complaints in,
    102
NFPA diamond indicator of hazardous
    material, 288
Nitroglycerin, administration of, 208,
    209
Orthopedic emergency, 98
Osteoporosis, 241
Oxygen delivery, 184–188
Oxygen-powered ventilator, flow-
    restricted, 179
Pancreas, 215
Pancreatitis, 83
Paradoxical motion, 185
Paraplegia, 275
Patient care report, 51, 53, 150, 177
    at mass casualty incident, 292
Patient information, 47
    confidentiality of, 15, 187
Patient transportation, 44, 170, 174,
    239, 264
    by air, 296
Pediatrics
    airway obstruction, 195
    assessment, 16
    chest compression, 214
    child abuse (*see* Child abuse)
    choking, treatment of, 136
    croup, 199
    epiglottitis, 137
    heart rates, of infants, 252
    respiratory distress, early signs, 134
    respiratory rate for infants, normal,
        31
    seizures, 65, 278
    stridor, 195
    treatment, 133
Pericardial tamponade, 131
Physical examination, 32
PMS, 36
Pneumonia, 194

Poisoning, 71–73
  Activated charcoal, 191, 222
  carbon monoxide, 74–76
  medication for, 72, 219
  poison control center, 226
  Syrup of Ipecac, administration of, 219
Pregnancy. *See also* Delivery; Labor
  abortion, spontaneous, 243
  assessment of, 99
  gestational length, 240
  labor, 97
  toxemia, 100
  transportation of patient, 139
  uterine rupture, 244
Protective gear, 295
  types of, 286
Protocols for EMTs, 182, 188
  for burn patients, 231
Psychological disorders. *See* Depression
Pulmonary edema, 196, 197
Pulmonary embolism, 60, 263
Pulse, 37
  assessment for, 167
Radiation, heat transfer by, 227
Radioactive incident, 141
Rescue breathing, 164, 213
Respiration, 39
  assessment of, 163
  oxygen delivery, 184–188
  suctioning, 19, 176
  tidal volume, 163, 164
Respiratory disorders, 56–58
  airway obstruction, 30, 195
  Albuterol, 193
  assessment of, 55
  hyperventilation, 198
  medications, administration of, 56
  medications for, 54, 194
  nasopharyngeal airway, insertion of, 178
  in pediatric patients, 102, 135
  pneumonia, 194
  pulmonary edema, 196, 197

pulmonary embolism, 60, 263
stridor, 29, 30, 195
Responding to a call, 49
Ribs, flailed segment, 35
SAMPLE history
  acronym, 169
  of trauma patient, 38
Scene safety, 74, 132, 135, 140, 149, 181, 221, 255, 280, 295
Seizures, 66, 67
  in pediatric patients, 65, 278
  status epilepticus, 278
  toxemia-related, 101
Sellick maneuver, 299
Septic shock, 256
Sexual assault, 130
Shock
  anaphylactic, 68, 218
  cardiogenic, 107
  hypotension, 253
  hypovolemic, 128, 254
  septic, 256
  stages of, 110
Shortness of breath, treatment of, 26
Shoulder, dislocation of, 121, 267
Sinoatrial node, 4
Skin, layers of, 166
Skull
  areas of, 161
  basilar fracture of, 122
Snake bite, treatment of, 92
Spinal cord injury, 126
  and paraplegia, 275
Splinting, 120, 269
Sprain, 265
  pre-hospital treatment of, 266
Status asthmaticus, 58
Status epilepticus, 278
Stressful situations, 157, 158
Stridor, 29, 30
  in children, 195
Stroke
  hemorrhagic, 63
  risk factors for, 290
Subdural hematoma, 271

Suctioning process, 19, 176
Suicide, 237
    risk factors for, 238
Syrup of Ipecac, administration of, 219
Tachypnea, 21
Terminal illness, emotional response to,
    11. *See also* Death, grieving process
Tidal volume of breath, 163, 164
Toxemia, 100
    seizures, 101
Transient ischemic attack, 62
Trauma
    to abdomen, 82
    assessment of, 10, 38–40, 127
    to brain, 270
    mechanism of injury, 171
    opening of airway, 18
    score, 40
    sexual assault (*see* Sexual assault)
    ventilation techniques in treatment
        of, 18, 22–24
Treatment, consent of, 13

Treatment release form, 52, 189
Tricuspid valve, 251
Tuberculosis, 12
Umbilical cord
    cutting at delivery, 245
    prolapsed, 246
Unconsciousness. *See also*
    Consciousness
    assessment, 7
    treatment of, 175
Uterus, rupture during pregnancy, 244
Ventilation, 18, 22–24
    and chest compression, 144
    flow-restricted oxygen-powered
        ventilator, 179
    gastric distention, prevention of,
        179, 180
    in intubated patients, 294
    nasopharyngeal airway and, 178
Violent patient, 91
Vital signs, 43

Due regard.